Beginners' Guide to

# JOURNALISM

&

## MASS COMMUNICATION

# BEGINNERS'
# GUIDE TO
# JOURNALISM
# & MASS COMMUNICATION

Barun Roy

PUSTAK MAHAL®

Delhi • Mumbai • Patna • Hyderabad • Bangalore

*Published by:*

# V&S PUBLISHERS

F-2/16, Ansari road, Daryaganj, New Delhi-110002
23240026, 23240027 • *Fax:* 011-23240028
*Email:* info@vspublishers.com • *Website:* www.vspublishers.com

### Regional Offi ce : Hyderabad
5-1-707/1, Brij Bhawan (Beside Central Bank of India Lane)
Bank Street, Koti, Hyderabad - 500 095
040-24737290
*E-mail:* vspublishershyd@gmail.com

### Branch Offi ce : Mumbai
Godown # 34 at The Model Co-Operative Housing, Society Ltd.,
"Sahakar Niwas", Ground Floor, Next to Sobo Central, Mumbai - 400 034
022-23510736
*E-mail* vspublishersmum@gmail.com

Follow us on: 

All books available at **www.vspublishers.com**

© Copyright: Author
**Edition 2015**

*Printed at :* Param Offseters, Okhla, New Delhi-110020

# DEDICATION

*This book is dedicated to my parents…*

*Without whose love and blessings, nothing would have been possible*

# Preface
### (To the first edition)

This book welcomes you to the exciting world of print journalism. The aim of this book is to help you gain a better understanding of the whole communication process and to demonstrate how to use words to convey ideas and expressions as well as facts effectively.

Once you have gone through this book, I am sure you will have a better understanding of your daily newspaper, and recognise it as a guardian to your country's freedom and a protector of your right to be fully informed.

You will acquire new insights into the phenomenon of mass communication and its effect on human beings. Because of your personal experience with other mass media, you will be better prepared to consider how these media can affect the lives of the people around the world, both, in a positive and a negative manner.

*Autumn, 2000*                                        **— Barun Roy**
*Rockville, Darjeeling*

# Preface
## (To the fourth edition)

Since the first, second and third editions were published, *Beginners' Guide to Journalism* has become popular as an effective introduction to Journalism. Enthusiasts throughout the country have commented favourably on its clear instructions and step-by-step approach to news writing and editing skills. It is not a surprise thence that a need for the fourth edition of the book was felt by both, the readers and the publishers. In these eight years since the book was first published, Journalism has, as a subject of study and career, flourished immensely. This edition thus intends to deal with the new aspects of Mass Communication.

Being the latest and updated version, this edition has infused marked improvements in all compartments to facilitate greater understanding and grasp on the subject and effectively contribute to the field of Journalism. The entire text has been revised and updated without essentially disturbing the main contents of the book. All sections essentially contain many more of the professional journalistic details, examples and terms than did the first, second and third editions.

The section on grammar – expanded and illustrated with clear, brief sample sentences – will provide helpful guidance to all readers in an area that many writers find difficult and confusing. The glossary has been upgraded and new terms have been added. Important issues like libel, makeup problems and modern techniques of editing have also been deliberated in detail. New sections on Radio and TV Journalism have been added to do justice to the completeness of the book. Further, Online or Internet Journalism and Blogging have been discussed in detail.

New examples of fine writing, superior photography, and outstanding page makeup from recent issues of some of the best newspapers in the world, including *The Times of India, De Standaard, Morgunbladid, La Nacion, Hindustan Times, Ole, Kathimerine, Bahrain Tribune, National Post, The Vancouver Sun, Toronto Star, China Daily*, etc. further enhance this edition.

All said and done, I thank the readers for accepting *Beginners' Guide to Journalism* with such whole-heartedness and hope that they will also receive this fourth edition with same enthusiasm.

Rest and all is the will of our Lord.


*Spring, 2008*                                                     **— Barun Roy**
*Clarke Road, Darjeeling*

# CONTENTS

# News, Views and You

## Mass Communication

In today's world, you are surrounded by ideas and information. They reach you in many ways and are intended to inform you, entertain you, or influence your thinking. Mass Communication is the name given to this process.

**Word formation**: Mass + Communication

## Mass

The term 'Mass' simply implies great volume, range or number of people.

## Communication

The communication process, however, implies numerous things. To begin with, any kind of communication, whether it be written or oral, or one that does not involve use of words, signs, signals, pictorials, body language, etc, must have a 'sender' and a 'receiver'. For a message to get through fully, there must also be a communicative spirit between the sender and the receiver in addition to the words or actions used to convey the message.

Thus, for Mass Communication to be achieved, the following parameters must exist:

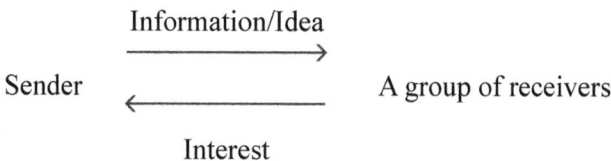

Information/Idea

———————————→

Sender     ←———————————     A group of receivers

Interest

Interest implies a definite interaction between the sender of the information/idea and the group of receivers. Without this very important aspect of mass communication, no message or information is relayed to the group of receivers and consequently mass communication is said to have failed. Generating and maintaining interest amongst the group of recipients – categorised differently as audiences, readers, surfers, etc. is one of the most important pursuits of a student of mass communication.

## How do we communicate?

Before the invention of language, our forefathers communicated with each other using gestures and through the medium of different sounds (drums etc.). Later, language brought them together and they started communicating verbally. Authors and poets wrote prose and poems and singers composed songs. They experimented with different sounds emanating from different objects and invented music. With the advent of industrial age, humanity was thrust into an era of technology and it became possible to relay spoken words, sounds, visuals – static or moving – amongst others.

The communication process today, thus, could involve written words or texts, drawings including diagrams, charts, artistic pictures, photographs, spoken words and sounds (audio), moving pictures (video) and animation.

*Communication in this advertisement relies on words and drawings* →

*Communication here relies both on words and pictures* →

## THE CATCH

### Chances of Miscommunication

As mass communication implies ideas or information being transmitted to a group of recipients, there always remain chances of miscommunication.

Miscommunication results when the message sent through a medium is received by a group of receivers in a distorted form. Miscommunication can also result from the incomplete relay of the message to the receiver. Further, the receiver himself or herself may interpret the message wrongly resulting in a miscommunication.

In the World Peace campaign logo given here, a simple spelling error has resulted in a critical miscommunication.

## How to avoid Miscommunication

The sender of the message who could also effectively be a writer must use words, diagrams or photos that convey his idea/message accurately.

Similarly, while writing articles or news items, the same writer must recognise that he can be influenced by his own feelings, his attitude towards his topic, and his past experiences. The writer must also recognise that when he applies words, he is using symbols that carry different shades of meaning. Therefore, he must employ language that is pertinent and effective in transmitting the true meaning of his message.

But this also implies that the writer's message cannot be communicated effectively unless the reader understands exactly what the writer is thinking and feeling. The reader, like the writer, is affected by his own attitudes and experiences, and he may therefore have a tendency to misunderstand or misinterpret the writer's ideas. Further, the reader may be unaware of his own misinterpretation of a message, or even of the reasons for his distortion of the real meaning of the message. Therefore, the writer must recognise his responsibility to write as clearly as possible.

However, communication can still exist to some degree even if the message is not conveyed under ideal conditions. Often mass communication depends on the assumption that at least some part of the message will generally be received, even if the receiver is paying little attention to it. For example, an advertisement with repetitive slogans, jingles, or concepts is based on this understanding.

**Mass Communication achieves several purposes**: to entertain, to inform and to influence attitudes, feelings or actions.

## Instruments of Mass Communication

The simplest way of spreading news is by word of mouth. One person tells another what he has seen or heard. This was also man's primal mode of communicating news, and this method is still in vogue to carry information about families, friends, or neighbourhood activities. Newsgathering methods developed and evolved to better levels gradually as the outlook of nations and governments changed, business and economies flourished and a far greater number of people started travelling from one part of the globe to another. Modern inventions such as printing press, ships, rail, road, airplane, telegraph, telephone, radio, television, Internet and satellite improved the speed with which news can be gathered and finally distributed. These inventions helped in transforming the world into a global village.

*Television is today one of the most popular instruments of Mass Communication in India*

Popular instruments of mass communication are radio, movies, pictures, books, newspapers, magazines, music and Internet.

Mass Media is also a term applied to the different instruments of mass communication.

## News

News is one of the most important and desired commodities furnished by mass media. People want to know what is going on around them. News connects them to the world and makes them aware of events that are taking place. News also makes people feel that they are a part of a bigger network of a people or in simple words a bigger community.

14

News, however, has a very short life. There is nothing more worthless and stale than yesterday's news. Hence, timing is one of the most crucial factors in news. News, if not delivered at an appropriate time, is simply not news.

Many of the instruments of mass communication considered in the following paragraphs are well fitted to accomplish this.

1.  **Live Broadcasts of Actual News Events**: Live coverage of events as they occur places the viewer as an eyewitness to sports events, important speeches, political meetings, and other newsworthy happenings. Generally, these broadcasts are planned in advance. Radio broadcasts of actual events have the same speed of transmission and lack only the picture on the screen.

    *Rob Riggle reporting live for CBS from Iraq*

2.  **News Reports**: Both Radio and Television feature frequent reports of current happenings all over the world. These are collected by the same news services that furnish information to newspapers, and the television channels frequently show 'Film clips' of the events taken at the time of their occurrence. Thus, those who may have missed the 'live' broadcast of an important

    *'News at 8' is a famous news programme of the KNBK Network in the United States*

    happening can see it when a portion of the earlier broadcast is repeated as part of regular news programme.

3.  **Documentaries**: Motion pictures of current events are often prepared for television showing. These may not present news

immediately after it happens. However, they often present background information and 'in-depth' coverage, not otherwise available.

*'TOP GEAR' is one of the critically acknowledged documentaries featured on BBC*

4. **News Magazines**: News magazines summarise, discuss, or interpret news events. Usually published weekly, fortnightly or monthly, they carefully organise and analyse the news and present it to their readers.

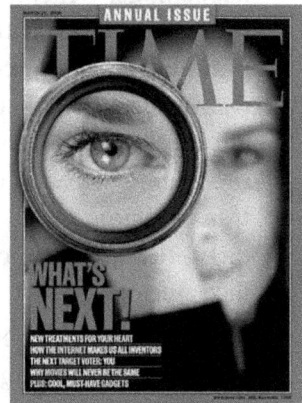

*Time is one of the most respected and successful magazines in the world*

In general, magazines also appeal to groups of people having special interests. More than half the magazines printed in the world serve readers interested in a particular profession, occupation, or hobby. Successful magazines enjoy fantastic circulation. The *Reader's Digest* has more than 25 million subscribers, while many other magazines distribute more than one million copies of each issue.

5. **Newspapers**: Daily or weekly newspapers furnish a written account of events which have just happened or are about to happen. Freshness of news is important to newspapers. They report the facts about an event with as much detail as can be collected in a short time.

Although newspapers reach their readers more slowly than Radio or TV, they have not suffered adversely from the competition.

Rather, a brief broadcast seems to generate the curiosity in listeners to read a more comprehensive report. Newspapers further have the advantage of being available whenever the reader wishes to pick them up. They also allow the reader to select the news stories that interest him and read them at will and devote time to them according to his leisure or preferences.

Consequently, newspapers remain the most important tool amongst the various news distributing media. Unlike other major instruments for spreading news, they combine speed and permanence.

## News Broadcasts

Although a comparatively new entrant in the communication scene, television has reached an impressive position among the mass media. Newspapers, magazines, and books have changed character as a result, although in most cases they have not severely suffered from the competition.

*Reading news for Television*

News Broadcasts owe their standards to newspaper traditions established over many years[1].

To begin with, it is important to distinguish between newscasts, the 'news pages' of the air, commentaries and the 'editorial pages'. National or international items for a newscast are provided either by their own reporting staff or by press agencies, while local news is covered and supplied by the reporting staff. Special editorial staff then prepare the news for broadcasting. News broadcasts have substantially the same privileges and practically the same limitations as newspapers. Hence, they should be listened to with this in mind.

---

[1] In fact, most of the news channels today in India and abroad are actually owned and managed by publishers who had earlier been or are still deeply rooted in Print Journalism. Aaj Tak owned by the India Today Group, MSNBC, Warner News, Sun Network, Star Groups owned by Rupert Murdoch and so on are a few examples. Even some TV channels, like the National Geographic run by the National Geographic Society is nothing but an electronic offshoot of the famous magazine with the same name i.e. *National Geographic* Magazine.

A commentator expresses his personal opinions about news just as a newspaper columnist does. He is presumably an expert, familiar with his field. Ideally, his comments are designed to ignite your thinking and cognitive powers.

On the other hand, electronic media rarely editorialise themselves in the sense of giving the opinions of the stations (channels). The major reason behind this position is the fact that stations need to be licensed by the government to avoid conflicts in the use of the airwaves. While the government has tried to encourage stations to present editorial opinion, they have been reluctant to do so primarily because of government control of their other activities, such as the regulation of the proportion of advertising to a certain ratio of the total programme time, the 'equal time' requirements for political broadcasts, and review of licence renewal.

□□□

# Different Kinds of Newspapers

In the previous chapter, I had deliberated upon the different instruments of mass communication. Newspapers are one of the most important and earliest instruments of mass communication. Newspapers have informed and entertained its readers since the times of Julius Caesar.

The main purpose of a newspaper is to inform its readers about current events, happenings of all kinds within the recent past or lend a peep into the events of the near future. Most newspapers also print advertisements in addition to diverse reading materials (comic strips, lifestyle, puzzles, human interest stories, etc.) that are not news but can be entertaining or informative.

There are many different kinds of newspapers, the most important of which are:

**Daily Newspapers**: They attempt to cover all kinds of news, i.e. news from different parts of the world as well as the important happenings in their own cities, communities, business, sports, society, and entertainment news. Generally, the front page of the daily is devoted to important events that have taken place during past 24 hours or that are to take place in the near future.

Almost every metropolis or large city in India publishes its own edition of daily newspapers. Dailies from major cities are widely distributed, often throughout states. They bring reports of every prominent happening as well as local news to their readers.

**Weekly Newspapers**: Covering local news is the main purpose of weekly newspapers published in small towns, suburbs, or community areas within cities. They specialise in the one news element that daily newspapers do not cover: detailed, personal news about people and events in their communities.

**Special Newspapers**: Organised groups such as engineers' society (e.g. Aeronautical Society of India, Institute of Engineers, Computer Society of India, etc.), labour unions, and large industries publish these for their members.

Many of these papers are published regularly and contain the information that concerns a limited group or a special situation.

**School Newspapers**: Like weekly newspapers, school, college or university papers serve the interest of their local communities – the 'community' in this case being the school/college/university itself. They may be published monthly, every two or three weeks, weekly, or even daily. They include news of past and present school events, articles about students and teachers, and frequently carry advertisements of interest to their readers. However, the practice of publishing school newspapers is not very popular in India, and college and university newspapers are also published in small numbers.

## How does a Newspaper serve the community?

The newspaper tries to keep its readers well informed about local, national and international affairs so that they may be 'kept posted' on current events, think intelligently, and form their own opinions about these matters. If we study newspapers from the point of view of what they are trying to do, we can discover three general areas of activity.

First, the newspaper presents news reports, as complete as possible in view of the limited time available for their preparation. Then comes expert opinions of correspondents, news analysts, and columnists concerning the news events. Finally, the newspaper states its opinion in the editorials. The influence of a widely read newspaper's editorials may be quite great, for people come to depend on these comments, especially when they do not have all the facts with them upon which to base their own decisions.

Secondly, the newspaper attempts to furnish up-to-date information about products, services, and activities which will make life better, more interesting, and more worthwhile for its readers. Many newspaper items serve this function. They include news about municipal projects on civic amenities, where to travel, and latest developments in science or medicine, as well as information and advertisements concerning material things that will make life more comfortable.

Finally, a newspaper carries some items solely for the purpose of entertaining its readers. News of unusual or humorous events, comic strips and cartoons, stories, puzzles, some daily columns, and similar items are both entertaining and relaxing.

□□□

# Different Kinds of Periodicals

Any printed material published between frequent and equal intervals or after stipulated period can be categorised as a periodical. Newspapers as such are arguably periodicals being published either daily or weekly. News Magazines are periodicals published weekly, fortnightly or monthly. However, periodicals as instruments of mass communication have now been more or less said to include all those publications that are published weekly, fortnightly or monthly, thus effectively excluding newspapers published daily.

Periodicals, unlike newspapers, do not deal with news reports on 'as it happens and when it happens' basis. Instead, they deal with in-depth analysis of what happened and what can happen in the future. Now, this in-depth analysis of issues at hand can be in reference to any interest – society, education, entertainment, career, technology, sports, etc.

Based on the periodicity of the publication and the subject, there are:

**News Magazines**: As discussed in the first chapter, news magazines summarise, discuss, or interpret news events. Usually published weekly, fortnightly or monthly, they carefully organise and analyse the news and explain it to their readers.

**Literary Magazines and Journals**: Literary journals publish news about authors, poets, books and publishing houses. They also publish short stories, poems, and literary criticism and discuss different issues concerning literature and litterateurs. A literary journal may not be for everyone but cater to those interested in literature.

**Technology Journals and Periodicals**: Our nation today boasts of some of the best technology journals and periodicals published in the world. Technology journals and periodicals, as the name suggests, deal with news, views and insights from and of technology, industry and scientific community in the nation. *Digit*, *PC Quest*, *Chip* are today some of the best IT-related Journals not just in India but in Asia as a whole.

**Religious, Spiritual and Linguistic Journals**: Religious and spiritual journals published monthly have recently become immensely popular in India. These periodicals, dedicated towards propagating the virtues of a religion, are basically targeted towards the members of the said religion. Similarly, linguistic journals of linguistic minorities in India, such as the Lepchas, Rais, Limbus, Nagas, Totos, etc. have also come into publication. While these linguistic journals may or may not have commercial objectivity, they work diligently towards the preservation of their language, script, literature, culture and traditions as a whole. These are community-driven enterprises and hence a community affair.

*Our Daily Bread*, is an example of a Christian Journal propagating the virtues of Christianity amongst Christians while *Aachuley*, is a respected linguistic journal of the Lepcha people.

**Film Journals**: Our country produces the largest number of movies in the world. As the largest producer of movies, our country is also home to the largest number of movie stars. Movie Magazines dedicated to bringing news and gossips of the film industry and the film stars are thus published regularly and in almost every language spoken throughout the nation.

**Music Journals**: The music industry in our nation is at par with the movie industry and as our movies are essentially musical melodramas, musicians, singers and music directors are always sought after. Our nation with her diverse culture and tradition also has deep-rooted music traditions that are as diverse as the people themselves. The close cultural ties with the Western world have further brought about an increase in the interest-factor generated in Western music. The result, a potpourri of musical traditions and interests has come into existence and therefore specialised music magazines are being published to cater to these interest groups that are popular not just among the young generation, but the music buffs from all age groups.

The most popular music magazines in the nation are *Rock Street Journal* and *Record*.

## Journals dedicated to Women, Teens and the Youth

Certain journals devoted to the interests and issues of different sections of the people are published regularly in the nation. These journals specifically dedicate themselves to issues related to women, and carry information, articles and interest-stories entirely on issues concerning women. While feminism may or may not be the editorial policy of these periodicals, girls, housewives or elder women is their targeted readership. *Femina* and *Cosmopolitan* amongst others are some of the most popular magazines dedicated towards women in the nation.

Based on the same philosophy, numerous magazines devoted towards highlighting the issues of the teenagers in the nation are published regularly in different cities. Some of the famed teens magazines are *Teens*, *Teenager* and *Wisdom*.

Apart from these periodicals, there are a number of other periodicals such as sports magazines, health magazines, hobby journals (interior decoration, gardening), neighbourhood journals, etc., which are published at regular intervals.

Television serials broadcast on the television channels are also modern forms of periodicals. These may entirely be entertainment oriented but they still come in the realm of mass communication. So do news reports broadcast through radio and television at regular intervals. *The World This Week* hosted by Prannoy Roy on *Doordarshan* was a famous television news periodical.

☐☐☐

# Films, Television and Radio as Instruments of Mass Communication

Film is not only a form of entertainment but also a powerful medium of mass communication. It is extensively used in publicity, public relations and advertising. A Mass Communication student, therefore, must study this medium as one of his or her tools to see how it can be applied. Hearing and seeing are the two important senses that have been bestowed upon us. Our capacity to retain any message enhances considerably when we hear and see it simultaneously. Thus, films are a powerful medium and can cast a momentous impact, for they enable the ideas to be seen and heard by the people at the same time.

## Advantages of Visual media

1. Ideas communicated through the films are retained longer than those received through other media of communication.

2. Films can transcend the barriers of illiteracy; even uneducated people can understand its theme.

3. Films are useful in motivating the people and help nation-building activities.

4. Films last long and some films have permanent value. With the help of a film, one can turn around the clock and peep into history and the past events.

5. Films provide a universal language and contribute to fostering a sense of oneness in a multilingual country. For instance, Bollywood

has contributed more towards unifying India through movies than any other industry or Government agencies, for that matter.

In short, like any other medium of communication, film serves the journalistic trinity of purposes: to inform, to influence and to entertain.

## Types of Films

Films are of different types:

1. **Feature Films**: These are the usual full-length commercial films being shown in the cinema houses.

2. **Documentary Films**: The Government, Public Sector Undertakings or private individuals produce these films for educating people.

3. **Children's Films**: They contain the themes that are of interest to children. The Children's Film Society of India produces such films. Interestingly, feature and animated children films have now become a popular genre in the Indian Film Industry.

4. **P. R. Films**: Commercial enterprises and other institutions produce these films. The main objective behind making Public Relations Films is to educate and inform the public about their organisations.

5. **Advertising Films**: Commercial firms produce these films to sell their products and services.

6. **Instructional Films**: They are intended for educating students in certain technical subjects and they are useful in educational institutions.

## Radio as a Medium of Mass Communication

Of all the instruments of mass communication, radio is one that carries the message around the world in the shortest possible time. It transcends all other media in speed. Radio, therefore, has been described as one of the most powerful social instruments of informing, educating and entertaining people. As a tool of Public Relations, its potency for opinion formation is strikingly singular. Most of the nationwide or statewide publicity campaigns begin with radio broadcasts. In a country like ours where still a majority of the population is illiterate, radio is a superb vehicle of communication for transmitting ideas.

The radio comes in the forefront of all the media of mass communication solely because of its unusual characteristics: its universality, its contemporaneous nature, its direct and individual appeal and its characteristic as a unique social instrument. The radio falls in the category of vocal communication system. And its impression is quick with immense grasp on the masses.

Radio offers certain services that are similar in nature to a newspaper. The services offered by the radio are:

1. It gives headlines in all news bulletins.

2. It has its own correspondents within the country and globally for reporting events.

3. It reviews books and presents comments on the news through commentators.

4. It provides features, interviews, stories, serials, etc.

5. It gives maximum sports coverage.

6. It carries advertising.

The basic difference between the radio and the newspaper is that the former appeals to the ear while the latter appeals to the eye. Radio reaches a larger mass of public than the reading public of newspapers.

## Television as a Medium of Mass Communication

As a medium of mass communication, television enjoys an unrivalled position. Possessing the immediacy of radio with the mobility of a cine-camera, it can make the best use of printed word, spoken word, motion picture, colour, music, animation and sound – all blended into one message. Its impact is more powerful than that of the radio or the printed word as it can command the attention of the eye as well as the ear. It has realism and nothing can be hidden from the inquisitive eye of the television camera. The TV has a useful role as an instrument of social change and can be used as an aid to the speedy socio-economic development.

Television had a late start in India in comparison to the rest of the world with an experimental TV centre established in 1959 in Delhi to telecast programmes of adult education. The centre was upgraded to a regular and fully accomplished station in August 1965. It has taken giant strides since offering entertainment, diverse information coupled with social education information.

□□□

# Radio in India

Radio broadcasts started in India in 1927 with two privately owned transmitters at Mumbai and Kolkata. The Government of India took them over in 1930 and the Posts and Telegraphs Department started operating them under the name of Indian Broadcasting Service. In 1936, the name of the service was changed to All India Radio[2] (also known as *Akashvani* since 1957) and it was made a separate department. At the time of Independence in 1947, All India Radio's network consisted of six radio stations. By 1982, it had 81 stations.

Programmes of music are broadcast from all stations of AIR and consist of classical, light classical, light folk, tribal and film music. A number of stations also air Western music. On an average, around 41 per cent of the total broadcasting time is devoted to music. Classical music, which was largely a preserve of *gharanas*[3] and princely courts in the pre-broadcasting period, has now become 'democratised' through AIR programmes and has evoked popular interest in forms and styles of India's ancient musical traditions.

## News Broadcasting

The News Services Division of AIR telecasts comprehensive and speedy coverage of news through its news bulletins, commentaries and discussions on current affairs. Besides noticing major trends in political, economic, social, cultural and scientific fields, it gives adequate attention

---

[2] Its acronym being AIR
[3] Broadly translated as houses or families who specialised in a special genre of classical Indian music

to parliamentary proceedings, rural development and sports activities. News is broadcast daily through 235 bulletins in 19 Indian and 25 foreign languages, and 34 regional dialects. Of these, 71 bulletins are beamed in the 'home service' from New Delhi and relayed by the other AIR stations. 106 regional bulletins are broadcast from regional stations and 58 bulletins are beamed to listeners abroad. The regional bulletins were introduced in April 1953. Specialised news bulletins carrying world news, sports news and state development news were introduced in 1974. Yet another feature of news coverage was the introduction of a news bulletin in Sanskrit.

Daily commentaries in English as well as Hindi review the day's proceedings in the Houses when the Parliament is in session. Commentaries by specialists in various fields and scripts from AIR's correspondents are broadcast in English and Hindi in the programmes called *Spotlight* and *Samayiki* respectively. In fact, now the entire proceedings of the Parliament in session are broadcast A special bulletin on *Question Hour in Parliament* is also broadcast. In the current affairs programme, specialists take up live issues for an intensive discussion every Sunday. Eyewitness accounts, interviews with important persons and reactions of the common man to the happenings around him are presented through radio newsreel in both English and Hindi.

### Transcription and Programme Exchange

The programme exchange and transcription service of AIR helps different stations to exchange programmes of outstanding value. The programme exchange and transcription service also transcribes the speeches of eminent personalities and maintains the library of Sound Archives. The collection consists of tape recordings and discs of a large variety of programmes. The Archive has a rich and valuable collection of some of the most historic audio records consisting of over 51 hours of recorded voice of Gandhiji, nearly 3000 tape recordings of Jawahar Lal Nehru's speeches having about 800 hours duration in addition to the voice tapes of Tagore, Netaji, Rajagopalachari and Sardar Patel.

Among other valuable items preserved are (1) recitations from the Vedas in Sanskrit in the traditional style, (2) poetry recitation by eminent poets in Hindi and other languages, (3) recitals by old masters of music, both Hindustani and Carnatic, (4) selected items of music by eminent musicians representing different *gharanas*, and (5) representative pieces of folk music, devotional music and stage songs. Some of the recordings of old maestros of music have been commercially released for music-lovers.

Radio is helpful in providing a greater variety of community voices – both of editorial and news worthiness. To be sure, too many of the broadcast editorials are still on 'safe' subjects, but here again it would appear that the older print medium has furnished the mould. Boldness hopefully will come with maturity.

□□□

# Television in India

Television is today recognised as the one of the most popular and powerful instruments of mass communication. Its effectiveness in relaying messages and information to the receivers is based on its ability to deal with news as it happens, when it happens and where it happens without loosing much time in its broadcast. In fact, live coverage of happenings has been made possible only by television. So much so that today, we can be a witness to happenings all across the world without ever having to leave our couch for a moment. This is mass communication at its finest. The power of television as an instrument of mass communication is also ascertained from the fact that no other medium is able to harness the power of audio and video as it does. While newspapers can only publish texts, diagrams and pictures, television can bring the news in all its glory, as it occurs.

## Television in India

Television first came to India as the National Television Network of India. It was named Doordarshan. The first telecast started on September 15, 1959 in New Delhi. For 13 years, there were no other stations until 1972, when the second television station was set up in Mumbai. By 1975, there were five more television stations based at Srinagar (Kashmir), Amritsar (Punjab), Kolkata (West Bengal), Chennai (Tamil Nadu) and Lucknow (Uttar Pradesh). For many years, the transmission was sourced in black and white. The television industry got the necessary boost in the eighties when Doordarshan introduced colour TV during the 1982 Asian Games.

## 1980s

The only television channel that existed in 1980s was Doordarshan, which was government owned. *Ramayana* and *Mahabharata* were the first major television series produced. These serials created new world records in terms of maximum numbers of viewership for a single programme. By the late 1980s, more people started owning television sets. Though there was a single channel, television programming had reached saturation. The government, hence, set up another channel that had partly national programmes on its list and partly regional. This channel was known as DD 2 or DD Metro. Both channels were broadcast terrestrially.

In 1991, Prime Minister Narasimha Rao launched a series of economic and social reforms. Under the new policies, the government allowed private and foreign broadcasters to engage in limited operations in India. All subsequent Central Governments and foreign channels like CNN, STAR TV and domestic channels such as Zee TV and Sun TV that have blossomed into media conglomerates have pursued this process consistently. Starting with 41 sets in 1962 and one channel (Audience Research unit, 1991), at present TV in India covers more than 70 million homes totalling a viewing population of more than 400 million individuals through more than 100 channels. A large relatively untapped market, easy accessibility of relevant technology and a variety of programmes are the main reasons for rapid expansion of Television in India. It must also be stressed that Television Entertainment in India is one of the cheapest in the world.

## Cable Television

In 1992, the government liberated its markets, opening them up to cable television. Five new channels belonging to the Hong Kong-based STAR TV gave Indians a fresh breath of life. MTV, STAR Plus, BBC, Prime Sports and STAR Chinese Channel were the 5 prime operating channels initially. Zee TV was the first private owned Indian channel to be broadcast over cable. A few years later, CNN, Discovery Channel and National Geographic Channel made their foray into India. STAR expanded its bouquet introducing STAR World, STAR Sports, ESPN and STAR Gold. Regional channels flourished along with a multitude of Hindi channels and a few English channels. By 2001, HBO and History Channel were the other international channels to enter India. By 2001-2003, Nickelodeon, Cartoon Network, VH1, Disney and Toon Disney joined the bandwagon. The boom of news channels started in the year 2003. Today, we have arguably the largest number of news channels in the world.

## CAS – Conditional Access System

CAS or conditional access system is a digital mode of transmitting TV channels through a set-top box (STB). The transmission signals are encrypted and viewers need to buy a set-top box to receive and decrypt the signal. The STB is required to watch only pay channels.

The idea of CAS was mooted in 2001, due to a furore over hike in charges by channels and subsequently by cable operators. Poor reception of certain channels, arbitrary pricing and increase in prices, bundling of channels, poor service delivery by Cable Television Operators (CTOs), monopolies in each area, lack of regulatory framework and redress avenues were some of the issues that were to be addressed by implementation of CAS.

It was decided by the government that CAS would be first introduced in the four metros. It has been in place in Chennai since September 2003, where it had managed to attract very few subscribers till recently. It has been rolled out recently in the other three metros of Delhi, Mumbai and Kolkata.

## DTH – Direct to Home

DTH is defined as the reception of satellite programmes with a personal dish in an individual home.

DTH does not compete with CAS. Cable TV and DTH are two methods of delivery of television content. CAS is integral to both the systems in delivering pay channels.

Cable TV is through cable networks and DTH is wireless, reaching direct to the consumer through a small dish and a set-top box. Although the government has ensured that free-to-air channels on cable are delivered to the consumer without a set-top box, DTH signals cannot be received without the set-top box.

□□□

# Internet as an Instrument of Mass Communication

If one is to even try to comprehend how Internet would change the very concept of mass communication as a whole in the mere five years to come, one would simply have to check his or her e-mail. In 2005, Google, the most famous of the search engines ever to bless the Internet offered free e-mail accounts with unlimited storage capacity. While the concept of unlimited space was reason enough for people to sign up for free e-mail accounts, Google offered an ingenious concept of Google Talk, Google Chat, E-mail Search and above all E-mail News. This meant that you could no longer just check your mails and ever need to delete it, you could chat with your friends, search for a small note in the heap of a million letters all the while reading the headlines and if needed the entire news. Google detected automatically the names of places typed and provided news and advertisements about that place. And if more information on any thing was required, one could simply search for it on the Internet by just typing in an input word. Google is after all the world's best search engine. Today, almost 72 per cent of the world uses Gmail and about 98 per cent use Google as the preferred search engine.

If what Google was able to achieve with Gmail were contemplated in the real world, it would essentially mean – (1) The Post Office offering you a post box of unlimited storage capacity free of cost for your entire life. (2) An official dedicated towards maintaining the records of your mail and who at the time of being asked about a letter received ten years earlier from an aunt present it to you, in almost a second in its pristine condition. (3) And the same official also being a general tracker of sorts who when asked of anything in the world comes up with every information on it that possibly exists. (4) And lastly, imagine an entire office or group of people working tirelessly to offer you information, including news, entertainment and gossips! And if all of these were indeed possible, it would have to be for free!

Certainly, such a thing had not even been thought of in 2000. Today, with high-speed Internet connectivity, movies, documentary and music videos despite their highest resolution can easily be watched on the Internet. The highest precision sound can only be accessed in the Internet. Internet makes it possible for a local village gossip to be heard side by side with the United States Presidential Address to the Congress. This is the true freedom of choice. Further, no government can bring down Internet. Nor can it be censored! It cannot be banned or held accountable. This does have a critical bearing on everything; the opportunities and the responsibilities nonetheless are seemingly limitless.

## The Unique Power of Internet

Internet today, has the unique ability to be as handy as the newspaper. You can simply connect or disconnect to the Internet at the stroke of a key, shut down the laptop or desktop and go to your work or do whatever you were doing previously. With the advent of laptop and the GPRS, Wide Area Network, and the LAN, or wireless Internet data modem, you can go online from any part of the world be it on the top of Mount Everest, at the toilet or while travelling — all the while doing your business. You can watch a movie, documentary or news report while being in a network with your friends wherever they are: in New York, Winnipeg, Sydney, Manila, Colombo, Chennai and Darjeeling enjoying and deliberating on the same as if they were physically present with you. You can also work simultaneously on many windows. Similarly, you can read news, cover stories, columns and comment on them and discuss with other members of the blog, discussion boards, news portal etc., making yourself heard across the world.

The most fascinating aspect of Internet is that it can be all the instruments of mass communication ever conceived without ever having to manifest the inherent weaknesses and shortcomings. For example, it can be a daily newspaper, where neither the publisher has to incur the daily expenditure of having to publish it or the reader of buying it. In essence, it is free for both the publisher and the reader[4]. The Internet can also access a radio or a television programme. While the surfer could listen or view the programme, he or she is ultimately free to choose. This freedom of choice is impossible to be achieved in Television or Radio. Even if one were to argue in regard to the number of channels and the scope of freedom of choice that surfing through them can offer, no one really knows today how many websites, Internet houses or that how many bulletin boards it has, which includes chat-lounges, networking sites, videos including live feeds and audios including live conversation. The physical size and the information that it offers is truly unfathomable.

## What is Internet?

The Internet is a worldwide, publicly accessible series of interconnected computer networks that transmit data by packet switching using the standard Internet Protocol (IP). It is a 'network of networks' that consists of millions of smaller domestic, academic, business and government networks, which together carry various information and services, such as electronic mail, online chat, file transfer, and the interlinked web pages and other resources of the World Wide Web (www).

The Internet and the World Wide Web are not one and the same. The Internet is a collection of interconnected computer networks, linked by copper wires, optic-fibre cables, wireless connections, etc. In contrast, the Web is a collection of interconnected documents and other resources, linked by hyperlinks and URLs[5]. The World Wide Web is one of the key services accessible via the Internet. However, 'the Internet' and 'the Web' are commonly used interchangeably in non-technical settings.

As of March 31, 2008, 1.407 billion people use the Internet according to Internet World Statistics.

---

[4] Of course, you might need to pay to access Internet today but the way the cost of Internet is coming down across the world, it is inevitable that it would one day be free.

[5] Uniform Resource Locator

## World Internet Users
## March 2008

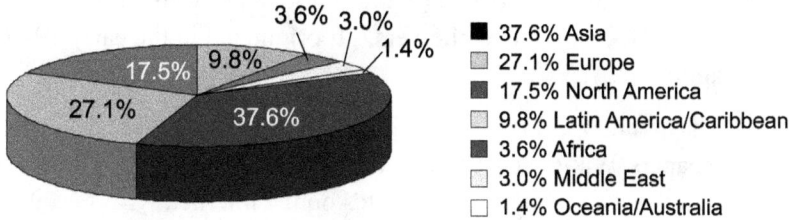

3.6% 3.0%
1.4%
9.8%
17.5%
27.1%
37.6%

- ■ 37.6% Asia
- ▨ 27.1% Europe
- ■ 17.5% North America
- ▨ 9.8% Latin America/Caribbean
- ■ 3.6% Africa
- ☐ 3.0% Middle East
- ☐ 1.4% Oceania/Australia

*Source: www.internetworldstats.com/stats.htm*
*Copyright © 2008. Mintwatts Marketing Group*

The following data will further show the power, strength and reach of the Internet in the different continents of the world.

## Internet Users in the World
## March 2008

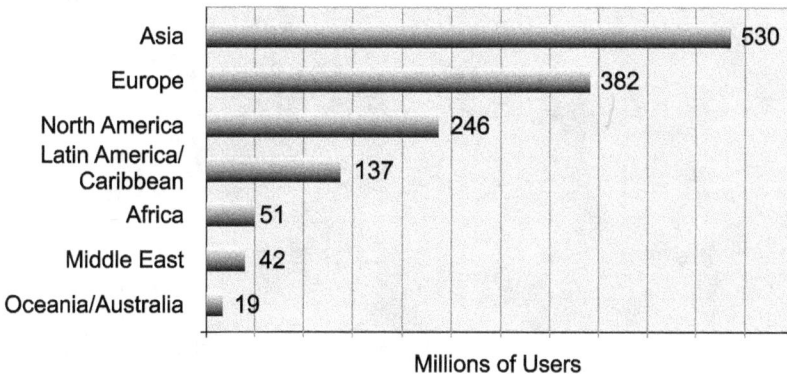

| | Millions of Users |
|---|---|
| Asia | 530 |
| Europe | 382 |
| North America | 246 |
| Latin America/ Caribbean | 137 |
| Africa | 51 |
| Middle East | 42 |
| Oceania/Australia | 19 |

Millions of Users

*Note: World Internet Users estimate is 1.,407,724,920 for Q1 2008*
*Copyright © 2008, Miniwatts Marketing Group-www.internetworldstats.com*

## Internet Journalism or Online Journalism

Internet Journalism, popularly known as online journalism, is defined as the reporting of facts produced and distributed via the Internet.

An early leader was *The News & Observer* in Raleigh, North Carolina. Steve Yelvington wrote on the Poynter Institute website about Nando, owned by The N&O, by saying "Nando evolved into the first serious, professional news site on the World Wide Web – long before CNN, MSNBC, and other followers." It originated in the early 1990s as "Nando Land".

Today, Yahoo, Google News, Topix, Wire, News Central, Live Art, E-newspapers, Wikipedia, Answers.com and MSN are some of the most respected news and entertainment sites on the internet.

Internet journalism operates like a daily newspaper and derives much of its journalistic heritage from print journalism.

□□□

---

[6] *The News & Observer* is the regional daily newspaper of the Research Triangle area of the U.S. state of North Carolina. The **N&O**, as it is popularly called, is based in Raleigh and also covers Durham, Cary and Chapel Hill. The paper also has substantial readership in the eastern portion of the state. It is the state's second-largest newspaper, after *The Charlotte Observer*. The paper has won three Pulitzer Prizes, most recently in 1996 for a computer-assisted investigation of the North Carolina hog industry.

# Introduction to Blogging

A web-log or just blog is the broad term applied to the online variant of the personal diary. Unlike diaries, blogs are intended to be public. Thanks to the ease with which blogs can be put online it has become one of the most powerful instruments of mass communication.

## Why do people Blog?

People blog for many reasons – some use it truly as an online diary, detailing their lives. Some blog to convey a message to the world especially when other media are not available or when revealing information through the usual channels would prove detrimental to their existence, as in the case of the Chinese bloggers[7]. Some use blogs to convey a message in a more informal manner than is possible through usual mass media channels, as in the case of politicians who use their blogs to reach out to their constituencies or organisations who reveal information about themselves that does not make it to mass media channels – like the internal working environment – which could be of interest to prospective employees. Information put up in a blog is seen as more sincere since it is shorn of all the trappings of a mass media presentation. This helps build a rapport with the targeted audience, which would probably explain why organisations encourage their employees to blog (with strict limits on what can be put online, of course).

---

[7] Since the Chinese Government severely censors news media, Chinese bloggers have found blogs to be the only way through which they could voice their dissent.

**Types of Blogs**

There are many different types of blogs, differing not only in the type of content, but also in the way that content is delivered or written.

1. **Personal blogs**: The personal blog, an ongoing diary or commentary by an individual, is the traditional, most common blog. Personal bloggers usually take pride in their blog posts, even if their blog is never read by anyone but them. Blogs often become more than a way to just communicate; they become a way to reflect on life or works of art. Blogging can have a sentimental quality. Few personal blogs rise to fame and the mainstream, but some personal blogs quickly garner an extensive following.

2. **Corporate blogs**: A blog can be private, as in most cases, or it can be for business purposes. Blogs either used internally to enhance the communication and culture in a corporation or externally for marketing, branding or public relations purposes are called corporate blogs.

Blogs can also be differentiated according to their genre and the technology used.

1. **By media type**: A blog comprising videos is called a vlog, one comprising links is called a linklog, a site containing a portfolio of sketches is called a sketchblog or one comprising photos is called a photoblog. Blogs with shorter posts and mixed media types are called tumblelogs. An Artlog is a form of art sharing and publishing in the format of a blog, but differentiated by the predominant use of and focus on Art work rather than text.

2. **By device**: Blogs can also be defined by which type of device is used to compose it. A blog written by a mobile device like a mobile phone or PDA could be called a moblog. One early blog was Wearable Wireless Webcam, an online shared diary of a person's personal life combining text, video, and pictures transmitted live from a wearable computer and EyeTap device to a web site. This practice of semi-automated blogging with live video together with text was referred to as sousveillance. Such journals have been used as evidence in legal matters.

3.  **By genre**: Some blogs focus on a particular subject, such as political blogs, travel blogs, house blogs, fashion blogs, project blogs, education blogs, niche blogs, classical music blogs, quizzing blogs and legal blogs (often referred to as a blawgs) or dreamlogs. While not a legitimate type of blog, one used for the sole purpose of spamming[8] is known as a Splog.

## The Blogosphere

The collective community of all blogs is known as the blogosphere. Since all blogs are on the Internet by their respective definitions, they may be seen as interconnected and socially networked. Discussions 'in the blogosphere' have been used by the media as a gauge of public opinion on various issues. A collection of local blogs is sometimes referred to as a bloghood.

## Blog search engines

Several blog search engines are used to search blog contents, such as Bloglines, BlogScope, and Technorati. Technorati, which is among the most popular blog search engines, provides current information on both popular searches and tags used to categorise blog postings. Research community is working assiduously to go beyond simple keyword search, by inventing new ways to navigate through huge amounts of information present in the blogosphere, as demonstrated by projects like BlogScope.

## Blogging Communities and Directories

Several online communities exist that connect people to blogs and bloggers to other bloggers, including BlogCatalog and MyBlogLog.

## Blogging and Advertising

It is common for blogs to feature advertisements either for the financial benefit of the blogger, or to promote the blogger's favorite cause. The popularity of blogs has also given rise to 'fake blogs' in which a company will create a fictitious blog as a marketing tool to promote a product.

---

[8] Spamming involves bombarding an individual with advertisement-oriented emails called spam.

## Popularity of the Blogs

Researchers have analysed the dynamics of how blogs become popular. There are essentially two measures of this: popularity through citations, as well as popularity through affiliation (i.e. blogroll[9]). The basic conclusion from studies of the structure of blogs is that while it takes time for a blog to become popular through blogrolls, permalinks[10] can boost popularity more quickly, and are perhaps more indicative of popularity and authority than blogrolls, since they denote that people are actually reading the blog's content and deem it valuable or noteworthy in specific cases.

### THE HIMALAYAN BEACON
http://www.beacononline.wordpress.com

| | |
|---|---|
| Technorati world ranking | -  469 754 |
| Number of blogs | - 50.75 Million |
| | |
| Alexa Website Ranking | - 794 267 |
| Alexa India Raning | - 60, 593 |
| | |
| Total number of website | - 156 Million |

*The Himalayan Beacon is presently rated as one of India's most upcoming blog.*

Researchers in the MIT[11] Media Lab launched the blogdex project to scroll the Web and gather data from thousands of blogs in order to investigate their social properties. It gathered this information for over four years, and autonomously tracked the most contagious information spreading in the blog community, ranking it by its regularity in posting and popularity. It can thus be considered the first instantiation of a memetracker[12]. The project is no longer active, but a similar function is now served by tailrank.com.

---

[9]  A blogroll is essentially a list of affiliated blogs
[10]  Short for Permanent Links
[11]  Massachusetts Institute of Technology
[12]  A software that tracks blogs

Blogs are given rankings by Technorati based on the number of incoming links and Alexa Internet based on the web hits. In August 2006, Technorati found that the most linked-to blog on the Internet was that of Chinese actress Xu Jinglei. Chinese media Xinhua reported that this blog received more than 50 million page views, claiming it to be the most popular blog in the world. Technorati rated Boing Boing to be the most-read group-written blog.

## Blogging Vs Mainstream Media – Redefining Journalism!

Many bloggers, particularly those engaged in participatory journalism[13], differentiate themselves from the mainstream media, while others are members of that media working through a different channel. Some institutions see blogging as a means of 'getting around the filter' and pushing messages directly to the public. Some critics worry that bloggers respect neither copyright nor the role of the mass media in presenting society with credible news. Bloggers and other contributions towards user-generated content[14] are behind Time magazine naming their 2006 person of the year as 'you'.

Many mainstream journalists, meanwhile, write their own blogs – well over 300, according to CyberJournalist.net's J-blog list. The first known use of a web log on a news site was in August 1998, when Jonathan Dube of The Charlotte Observer published one chronicling Hurricane Bonnie.

## The Consequences of Blogging

The emergence of blogging has brought a range of legal liabilities and other unforeseen consequences.

---

[13] **Participatory journalism**, also known as public or citizen journalism, is the act of citizens "playing an active role in the process of collecting, reporting, analysing and disseminating news and information," according to the seminal report *We Media: How Audiences are Shaping the Future of News and Information,* by Shayne Bowman and Chris Willis. The authors further write, "The intent of this participation is to provide independent, reliable, accurate, wide-ranging and relevant information that a democracy requires." Citizen journalism should not be confused with civic journalism, which is practised by professional journalists. Citizen journalism is a specific form of citizen media as well as user-generated content.

[14] Where most of the information is generated by the users, here readers.

Several cases have been brought before the national and international courts against bloggers concerning issues of defamation or liability. The courts have ruled mixed verdicts. Here are the examples of some of the most famous blogging controversies in India and abroad.

The IIPM controversy is known today, as one of the first Blogging Controversies to have ever taken place in India.

The IIPM controversy kick-started when an article, written by the then JAM writer Arjun Ravi was published in JAM magazine, edited and published by Rashmi Bansal. The article was an in-depth look at the claims that IIPM (Indian Institute of Planning and Management, an MBA Institution of repute in India) made in its press advertisements. Incidentally, the piece did not raise much controversy when it was first published. Gaurav Sabnis, who published Vantage Point, posted this article in his blog with a link to the article on the JAM website. Officials at IIPM read the post on Sabnis's blog. Sabnis, who at the time was working with IBM, was forced to quit his job after IIPM officials threatened to burn IBM laptops. The event caused uproar in the Indian Blogging Community who rushed to the support of both Sabnis and Bansal.

In the United States, Traffic Power sued blogger Aaron Wall for defamation and publication of trade secrets in 2005. According to Wired Magazine, Traffic Power had been 'banned from Google for allegedly rigging search engine results'. Wall and other 'white hat' search engine optimisation consultants had exposed Traffic Power in what they claim was an effort to protect the public. The case was watched by many bloggers because it addressed the murky legal question of who's liable for comments posted on blogs. The case was dismissed for lack of personal jurisdiction, and Traffic Power failed to appeal within the allowed time.

In January 2007, two prominent Malaysian political bloggers, Jeff Ooi and Ahiruddin Attan, were sued by pro-government newspaper, *The New Straits Times Press*. The Malaysian government supported the plaintiff. Following the suit, the Malaysian government proposed to 'register' all bloggers in Malaysia in order to exercise better control over parties working against their interest. This was the first such legal case against bloggers in the country.

In the United Kingdom, a college lecturer contributed to a blog in which she referred to a politician (who had also expressed his views in the same blog) using various uncomplimentary names, including referring to him as a 'Nazi'. The politician found out the real name of the lecturer (she wrote under a pseudonym) via the ISP and successfully sued her for £10,000 in damages and £7,200 costs.

## Political Consequences

Blogging can sometimes have unforeseen consequences in politically sensitive areas. Blogs are much harder to control than broadcast or even print media. As a result, totalitarian and authoritarian regimes often seek to suppress blogs, or to punish those who maintain them.

In Singapore, two ethnic Chinese were imprisoned under the country's anti-sedition law for posting anti-Muslim remarks on their web logs.

Egyptian blogger Kareem Amer was charged with insulting the Egyptian president Hosni Mubarak and an Islamic institution through his online blog. It was the first time in the history of Egypt that a blogger was prosecuted. After a brief trial session that took place in Alexandria, the blogger was found guilty and sentenced to a term of three years in prison for insulting Islam and inciting sedition, and one year for insulting Mubarak.

Egyptian blogger Abdel Monem Mahmoud was arrested in April 2007 for anti-government writings in his blog. Monem is a member of the banned Muslim Brotherhood.

After expressing opinions in his personal web log about the state of the Sudanese armed forces, Jan Pronk, United Nations Special Representative for the Sudan, was given three days notice to leave Sudan. The Sudanese army had demanded his deportation.

## The Impact of Blogging

Since 2002, blogs have gained increasing notice and coverage for their role in breaking, shaping, and spinning news stories. The Iraq war saw bloggers taking measured and passionate points of view that go beyond the traditional left-right divide of the political spectrum. On December 6, 2002 Josh Marshall's talkingpointsmemo.com blog called attention to U.S. Senator Lott's comments regarding Senator Thurmond. Senator Lott was eventually forced to resign over the matter.

As an example of the rise of importance of blogs, let me relate an incident. In 2002, many blogs focused on comments by U.S. Senate Majority Leader Trent Lott. Senator Lott, at a party honouring U.S. Senator Strom Thurmond, praised Senator Thurmond by suggesting that the United States would have been better off had Thurmond been elected president. Lott's critics saw these comments as a tacit approval of racial segregation, a policy advocated by Thurmond's 1948 presidential campaign. This view was reinforced by documents and recorded interviews dug up by bloggers. Though Lott's comments were made at a public event attended by the media, no major media organisations reported on his controversial comments until after blogs broke the story. Blogging helped to create a political crisis that forced Lott to step down as majority leader.

Similarly, blogs were among the driving forces behind the 'Rathergate Scandal', where (television journalist) Dan Rather presented documents (on the CBS show 60 Minutes) that conflicted with accepted accounts of President Bush's military service record. Bloggers declared the documents to be forgeries and presented evidence and arguments in support of that view, and CBS apologised for what it said were inadequate reporting techniques. Many bloggers view this scandal as the advent of blogs' acceptance by the mass media, both as a news source and opinion and as means of applying political pressure.

In the month of May 2008, The Himalayan Beacon, a blog maintained by this author posted news where the National Geographic Channel had called the traditional weapon of the Gorkhas 'infamous'. The post at the Himalayan Beacon resulted in a global outrage leading to a public apology by the National Geographic Channel.

□□□

# Introduction to Freelance Journalism

A freelance journalist is essentially a writer who is not attached to any newspaper or journal. He fends or works for himself and is not on the regular staff of any organisation. A freelance writer retains his independent identity and can write for different newspapers or journals. His articles and features are accepted on the basis of their standard of writing, suitability and demand. In fact, the name and personality of a freelance journalist counts a lot in the acceptance of his articles. If he is a famous person or an authority on a subject, his articles will be sought after by many newspaper and journals. On the other hand, if he is an unknown person, he will face a lot of difficulties in selling his articles.

A freelancer, of course, has the freedom to write for any number of newspapers, magazines, and on any subject. He may write on economics, sports, business, industry or any topic of human interest. He may write for one newspaper or journal on one subject, or for another on quite a different subject. Sometimes, a freelancer who contributes to some newspaper or magazine regularly becomes a popular person. A regular contribution is called a 'column' because it occupies a set space in a newspaper.

Undoubtedly, for an unknown freelancer, it is very difficult to earn his livelihood from journalism itself. Those who move to freelance writing after serving on the staff of some famous newspaper or magazine are in a much better position, because, while in service, they come to know the working of the newspapers thoroughly and can also develop very good contacts within the media. They may not have much difficulty in selling their articles. This is a fact that a freelance journalist has to struggle very hard in the beginning to establish himself or herself in this highly competitive profession.

A freelance journalist cannot afford the time and effort to write an article without prior demand on the chance that it may be accepted by some or the other newspaper, because, if by chance that article is not accepted, it will be a sheer waste of his resources, labour and time. He has to write such articles as are readily accepted by editors, so that he does not have to starve. For this purpose, he must know the requirements of each newspaper and magazine, so that he can write articles and features that are acceptable to them.

A freelancer must try to have good contacts with the editors of newspapers and magazines as well as with those who have the authority to accept his articles. He must also write continuously so as to keep himself in the public eye all the time. A freelancer should never depend only on one magazine, newspaper or periodical, because if he keeps all his eggs in the same basket, then he may face a lot of financial hardship, when that single source no longer needs him.

A freelancer should keep the latest addresses and telephone numbers of the important newspapers and magazines handy. He should try to have regular contacts with the concerned people of those magazines. He must have a systematic schedule of working. Being a freelancer does not mean that he should waste his time in an irresponsible manner. On the other hand, he must utilise every minute of his time to the best of his abilities, as his time is highly valuable. He should allot some time for researching new information and writing his articles, and some time for maintaining his contacts with the newspaper media.

A freelancer has more scope and demand in magazine journalism than in daily newspapers, because the magazines are generally understaffed and most of the articles and features they publish are invited from outsiders. The magazines are always on the look out for good and readable articles of general human interest. If a freelance journalist can offer them well-written, accurate and well-researched articles according to their requirements, then he might be in a position to develop extremely cordial, rewarding and fruitful relations with them. But he must deliver his articles before the deadline set by the editors of these magazines.

## Writing as a Critic

Writing critical analysis on various issues is one of the most important facets of freelance journalism and all newspapers devote much space to criticism of arts like films, books, music, theatre etc. A critic visits theatres, cinemas, art galleries etc. and after seeing the live performances or shows, writes a critical appreciation about them. Many people are very fond of reading the critic-columns in respect to drama, film, art show etc. These critics play a very important role by highlighting the good and adverse points of the shows that are running in the cities. Critics measure these shows on their standards of excellence and give their opinions.

Sometimes, the very success of a theatre, film or art show depends upon the favourable or unfavourable criticism that it receives in the press. A critic should be balanced in his approach and objective in his critical appreciation. He should not be vindictive or guided too much by his personal prejudices. A critic, first of all, should explain as to what a show is about, its contents or the story, and then he should point out its weak and good points. On the basis of his experiences, he can highlight its excellent features or criticise its anomalies.

## Criticism of Theatre

Many a time, the critic can mould or sway public opinion regarding shows favourably or unfavourably even as it is staged in a city for the first time. It is said that a critic can make or break a new show on its inaugural staging or premier screening on the first day. The star-cast of every theatrical staging aspires to know the comments they have received in the press. There is no doubt that the critic wields a considerable power as far as failure or success of a theatrical show is concerned.

A critic should remember the given points while filing his comments:

1.  He must keep in mind the audience for whom he is writing and what they are likely to enjoy.

2.   He should maintain widely accepted norms and standards of rating the performance levels and accordingly adjudge if the show can be classified as good or bad.

3.   He must highlight the finer points and aspects of the performance of a new show in clear terms, so that the readers can know whether they will enjoy it or not.

4.   A critic should try to know not only the tastes of the refined class and the art fraternity but also the liking of the masses.

5.   He should be able to comprehend the intricacies of both, a tragedy as well as a comedy, and thereby rate the show weighing all the aspects and nuances of art.

6.   He should always mark the performances of amateurs and professionals and amateurs from different perspectives because amateurs cannot be judged by the same yardstick that is used to judge professionals.

7.   A critic should not be swayed by his word spinning power and personal prejudices. He should not attempt to destroy a play by adverse comments merely to demonstrate his power.

8.   The criticism should be objective, well balanced and honest.

The critics of national newspapers have to work very hard. They are required to see a number of performances which, at times, can come up to one per night the whole week through in the prime season. After every performance, they have to rush to write their comments, so that the same appear in the next day's newspaper.

## The Film Critic

Generally, special shows of new films are screened for the media and film critics. Every national newspaper hosts a special column for film criticism, which is generally published once or twice a week, and especially on weekends or Sundays. When a particularly noteworthy film is released, a critic may be asked to review the film. There is a little difference between a theatre performance and a film. The theatre is a live performance in which a different mood and effect may prevail in every performance. Sometimes, even the leading players may be replaced. On the other hand, the film remains the same for every show, as it is a completely finished product. That is, a film show remains the same, even if it is seen after months or years.

A film critic should remember the following points:

1. He must be able to understand and assess various techniques of film making like acting, direction, photography, story line, locations etc.

2. The film critic should be aware of the productions of famous directors and producers.

3. He should also be conversant with the famous actors and actresses.

4. He should give a true assessment of a film, which should be objective and clear cut.

5. He can also inform his readers whether a film is average, below average, mediocre or excellent.

6. He should give a brief description of the story of the film, discuss the quality of music and rate the acting of individual actors and actresses.

## The Book Critic

Many writers have the feeling that the book critics hardly read their books before writing the reviews. They believe that the critics write their reviews only by reading the blurb and the few descriptive sentences inside the dust jacket. But this is not always correct. Of course, the authors sometimes do get this impression that either due to less space in the newspaper or due to the critic being overworked, a very sketchy review of their book is published.

There are generally three types of book reviews published in the newspapers:

1. Firstly, there is the essay type. It is a review that is comparatively longer written by an authority on the subject.

2. The second is a short review, which is given once a week in the review column by a reviewer who reviews a number of books.

3. The third is a sort of feature article that is put together from the contents of the book without giving any detailed judgement on it. A reporter generally writes this in the manner of a news story.

Hundreds of books get published every week. An author should be quite elated if even a small mention of the book is made in the book review column which usually gets published once a week. When a reviewer has been assigned more than one book on the same subject, he would usually review the most outstanding work in the beginning and comment upon others in the tail end. Usually, the new titles are sent to the newspaper offices a month or so before the official date of publication. A slip is also sent along with the book on which the title of the book, the name of the author, the price and the publication date are mentioned. Before writing the review of the book, the reviewer should write the name of the book, the name of its publisher, the name of its author, price of the book and the official date of the publication.

Book review should not be done in a superficial manner, but the reviewer should read the book thoroughly and give his opinion frankly in an objective and responsible manner.

## The Music and Art Critic

Generally, musicians and artists regard their critics as 'insensitive idiots'. There is no doubt that criticism of music and arts requires a lot of skill and experience, because here the critics have to find words to express the ethos of something that is in its essence so fascinating and profound. Only those who are knowledgeable about the different streams and branches of music and arts and have a great mental inclination and passion towards art and culture should become an art critic. Generally, the critics make it a point to use decent and subtle terminology to criticise music and art. Of course, the critic should be fair and accurate in his criticism. Musicians, artists and singers are extremely sensitive with a high emotional quotient; therefore, the critics should always use decent restraints when criticising their performances.

## Qualities of a Good Critic

To become a good critic, a person must develop aesthetic qualities in his writing to make it distinct and readable. He must always remember that both, the readers who are interested in the subject as well as those who are not will read his criticism. Therefore, he should write in such a manner that even those who are not interested in the subject would enjoy reading his criticism. Its readers enjoy a good criticism in seeming that they have themselves read the book or seen the play. In fact, a good critic shares his personal experiences with his readers. There are many persons who simply enjoy reading the review of a book or a music concert or a film. There are many others who would buy the book or go to see the film after reading the reviews in the press.

Thus, good criticism is a part of good journalism. The opinions of the popular critics are highly valued and respected. In the beginning, a young journalist may have to face some hindrances and problems to become a successful and popular critic. But fame cannot be achieved without doing hard work in any field. The same is true as far as journalism is concerned. The most essential quality of a critic is that he should be able to write something that is readable. Of course, he must also give a bird's eye view of the subject under review. The best critic is a person who can write the best readable prose.

□□□

# Freedom of the Press

We have already discussed the objectives of a newspaper and its role in the society. However, it is important to understand that all this depends on the freedom of the press[15].

Freedom of the press means the right to publish books, pamphlets, or newspapers without having to submit them in advance for government approval. The same freedom applies to cinema, television and radio. The writer is, of course, subject to punishment if he publishes false, scandalous, or malicious materials that are libellous in nature. However, this also implies that freedom to print and criticise is meaningless unless journalists have access to all pertinent facts about the world, and about what governments and organisations are doing. In practice, therefore, freedom of the press has been extended to mean 'freedom of information' that is, the right of the people of a free nation to be fully informed about affairs of national or local interest.

As with any privilege that affects other people's right, freedom of the press is subject to certain limitations and responsibilities to ensure its proper use. Some of these are as discussed below:

- **Ethics**

  Newspapers are commercial enterprises, usually owned and published by members of our own community. Like most Indian businessmen, these publishers want to serve the community

---

[15] Press in journalism often implies printing, a printing organisation or newspapers and periodicals collectively.

honestly, and at the same time make a fair profit. Generally, they want to keep up to the good reputation that they have painstakingly earned over a period of time.

All newspapers have written or unwritten standards about what to print. There are many 'taboo' topics that no respectable newspaper will report in its columns.

## • Libel

Freedom of the press exists as long as a newspaper uses the freedom with good motives and for desirable purposes but it can be regulated to guarantee that the focus of press remains within these parameters. The major weapon of control is the law of libel.

### What is Libel?

Perhaps the most frequently quoted definition of Libel is as given in the Illinois Criminal Code which says, *"A malicious defamation, expressed either by printing or by signs, pictures or the like tending to blacken the memory of one who is dead or to impeach the honesty, integrity, virtue or reputation or publish the natural defects of one who is alive, and thereby to expose him to public hatred, contempt, ridicule or financial injury."*

Libel occurs when a statement unjustly exposes someone to hatred, makes him seem ridiculous, or damages his reputation or earning power. The offended person may sue the writer or publisher for damages. The punishment can be imprisonment if the offence is extremely serious.

It is no wonder that editors and reporters are careful about what they print. However, once a statement has been circulated, the damage has been done. No apologies will change the fact that it was published and brought to public notice. Even proving such charges untrue rarely helps a person whose reputation has been injured.

### o *Civil and Criminal Libel*

'Civil' libel has been mentioned above and makes an important distinction that can no longer be postponed. Defamation through printing, etc., can be said to have two major kinds of effect with which the law is concerned. One is to cause injury to the individual member of society. The other is to cause injury to the society as a whole. The first of these is covered by civil libel. In such cases, the law allows the injured party to go to Court and obtain redress for his injury. Like all civil actions, the matter is between the first party and the second, with the public only providing the means, through the courts, of 'refereeing' the contest. In a criminal action, the public, having been wronged, acts directly through the courts to exact punishment.

It follows that the kinds of defamation that might result in injury to the public on the one hand or injuries to individuals on the other might be quite different. Without examining these differences in detail, it can be said that defamations which have a tendency to cause a breach of the peace fall into the criminal category, while those which tend to cause injury or suffering to an individual constitute civil libel.

On the other hand, when a publication defames a dead person, action is possible only through criminal libel because it has been held that the reputation dies with the person, which further means that no civil action is possible. The defamation, however, does not extend to his descendants, for instance, since it is his memory that has been blackened, not their reputations. Likewise, a member of an organisation cannot obtain redress when that organisation is ridiculed or falsely accused except in the rare case where he can show that he himself has somehow been identified. However, criminal action is possible in such a case, although such actions are rarely implemented. Malice is not assumed in criminal libel and must be shown.

○ **Per Se or Per Quod**

It now becomes necessary to make another distinction in 'types' of libel. In past decisions, courts both in India and the world have held certain words to be libellous in and of themselves, whenever applied to any person. These are libellous *per se*.

However, dangerous publications are not limited to such words. Others who may be innocent in themselves can prove to be dangerous in certain contexts. These are known as libels *per quod*. The precise legal distinction is not crystal clear but for our purposes it need not be. It serves to call attention to the fact that one needs to look beyond the mere word in assessing the libel hazard. It reminds us that innocuous words may be extremely dangerous owing to the way they are used. It is not libellous to say of a married woman that she gave birth to an either-pound boy but to say so falsely in the second month after marriage is another matter.

The distinction under discussion has another important aspect when and if the case comes to Court. Because libel *per se* is obviously defamatory, it is not necessary for the plaintiff to show that in some specific way he has in fact suffered as a result of the publication. Libel *per quod*, on the other hand, requires proof that special damages were suffered.

- **Right to Privacy**

  Publication of information about someone's private life might be cause for Court action against a newspaper. However, since laws do not cover people who place themselves before the public, determination of what is private and what is not becomes in most cases, a matter of newspaper ethics. Newspapers cannot pry into a citizen's private affairs, but if he does something newsworthy, he loses his right to privacy, because information about his action is a matter of public interest.

- **Censorship**

  Censorship of the press means inspection and approval of newspaper copy before publication. This simply means that censorship is based on the idea that some specific authority knows best what the public should read.

  Indian newspapers are not subject to government censorship during times of peace, except in certain matters affecting public morals, such as the publication of vulgar or obscene matter. However, information about the movements and activities of the armed forces is kept a closely guarded secret by the government to keep military facts out of militants' hands, especially in States like Jammu and Kashmir and North-Eastern India. Newspapers are also expected to avoid publishing articles that might give rise to a feeling of alienation to the minorities.

Newspapers frequently practise voluntary self-censorship and self-restraint particularly when they realise that the information that they hold about a particular happening is not in the public interest to publish. For instance, a newspaper may cooperate in withholding news about a kidnapped baby while the police search for the baby without the kidnappers' being aware of their movements. Then, the paper after the arrest of the kidnappers may lift its own censorship and can publish the entire story.

News from some foreign countries, even when written by Indian correspondents, is carefully scrutinised before it is released, as it may include half-truths.

Information on any intricate issue of national or state importance is closely held and concealed by Central or State Governments. Governments, in such a scenario, may hold secret meetings or executive sessions that are closed to reporters or vital news items may simply not be released. Many officials believe that it is their duty to protect the public by withholding certain information from publication[16]. However, the attitude of Indian newspapers is that citizens have the right to know what their government is doing, if they are to make intelligent judgements and remain a free lot.

---

[16] The Indian Right to Information Act (RTI Act) was introduced in the Indian Parliament in July 2000. It came into effect on 12 October, 2005. The Supreme Court of India had, in several judgements prior to enactment of RTI Act, interpreted Indian Constitution to read Right to Information as the Fundamental Right as embodied in Right to Freedom of Speech and Expression and also in Right to Life. RTI Act laid down a procedure to guarantee this right. Under this law all Government Bodies or Government funded agencies have to designate a Public Information Officer (PIO). The PIO's responsibility is to ensure that information requested is disclosed to the petitioner within 30 days or within 48 hours in case of information concerning the life and liberty of a person. The law was inspired by previous legislation from select States (among them Maharashtra, Goa, Karnataka, Delhi etc)

- **Copyright**

    Copyright, the right of authors or artists to prevent others from copying their original work without permission, may affect newspapers by limiting publication of interpretative material. Although most news stories are not covered by copyrights, some are. Such copyrighted exclusive stories may be carried by one newspaper but not by others. Newspapers may not reprint from books or magazines without permission, regardless of how pertinent the material might be to current problems and how it might help readers gain an understanding of current events.

- **Influence of Advertisers**

    Since advertisements pay most of the publishing cost of a newspaper, an editor or publisher must consider the possibility that advertisement might be withdrawn from his newspaper if it does not please the readers. In practice, most editors publish what they feel is right, not what their advertisers want them to and most advertisers are quite willing to allow newspapers to determine what news items to publish, and how to present these items to increase the circulation.

    But an omnipresent threat does exist that pressure by advertisers could sway a newspaper's standards, since the paper is, after all, a profit-making business venture.

that allowed the right to information (to different degrees) to citizens about activities of any State Government body.

A number of high profile disclosures revealed corruption in various government schemes such scams in Public Distribution Systems (ration stores), disaster relief, construction of highways etc. The law itself has been hailed as a landmark in India's drive towards more openness and accountability.

However, the RTI in India has certain weaknesses that hamper implementation. There have been questions on the lack of speedy appeal to non-compliance to requests. The lack of a central PIO makes it difficult to pinpoint the correct PIO to approach for requests. The PIO, being an officer of the relevant Government institution, may have a vested interest in not disclosing damaging information on activities of his/her Institution, This, therefore, creates a conflict of interest. In the state of Maharashtra, it was estimated that only 30% of the requests are actually realised under the Maharashtra Right to Information act. The law does not allow disclosure of information that affects national security, defence, and other matters that are deemed of national interest.

- **Influence of Readers**

  Circulation is the lifeblood of a newspaper. Although actual revenue from sales and subscriptions is small compared to the revenue from sales and advertising, it is circulation that makes advertising profitable. Increased circulation brings more advertisements and consequently, a newspaper aims at the largest circulation possible. The newspaper that prints what its readers want, sells its papers. Unfortunately, readers may prefer an emphasis on sensational news, rather than the more intelligent balance of all kinds of news that many editors would prefer to print.

## Readers' Responsibility

A free press may publish much of what would not get printed if the government controlled newspapers. Most editors and writers recognise a duty to their community and their readers. To the best of their ability, they report the news fairly, truthfully, and completely, yet there are ways in which they fail. Journalists are human beings with human feelings, and there are times when their own prejudices unwillingly creep into their reporting.

The whole responsibility, however, does not lie with the newspaper. If you, as a reader are not discerning and intelligible, you may fail to understand what a newspaper is trying to convey. Along with the privilege of receiving uncensored news, you must accept the responsibility of reading carefully. The following steps show you what to consider as you read the news. You must, of course, consider the same points when you listen to someone speak, in person, on radio, on television, or in motion pictures.

1. **Recognise and Understand Opinion**

   Opinion appears in every newspaper. Editorials are opinion, so are daily columns, plays and movie reviews, printed quotations or speeches. In all of these, it is clear whose ideas you, as a reader, are receiving. Editorials state the opinion of the newspaper itself. Columns and reviews have by-lines and contain the writer's comments. Any news story with a by-line may include the opinion of the report, although the by-line may be printed simply as credit for an outstanding piece of factual reporting. In addition, comments may be expressed in news stories, if they are properly placed within quotes or follow a phrase in the direct narration/speech, like Mr. Sharma says, "............."

Most newspaper readers want and welcome opinion, when it is clearly identified because it helps them weigh the news and form their own opinions. But their ojective and yours too must be to clearly understand the difference between fact and opinion.

## 2. Distinguish between Fact and Opinion

To a reporter, anything that really happens is a fact. If someone makes a statement concerning an event, the only known fact is that he talked. What he said must be considered his own personal opinion until it is clearly established that he was describing what actually happened. The reporter on call notes what was said, being careful to name the source. If the reporter has reason to believe that the statement is incorrect, he may qualify it in some way, perhaps with words like 'assert' or 'allege'. He may obtain contradictory statements from other sources. But he reports them just the same.

Here, the responsibility for determining the truth shifts to you, the reader. To understand what actually happened, you must analyze the statements in the story. You must make a distinction between actual facts and personal opinions. Moreover, you must watch for conclusions that someone has drawn. These are also opinions. Each time you find an opinion, identify it. Then consider it – whether to accept or reject it, then place it in the proper corner of your mind to assist in forming your own judgement about the news event.

## 3. Consider Each News Source

Another distinction that you as a newspaper reader must make is between facts and rumours or personal conclusions that may be stated as facts. Most newspapers identify their news sources by name or indicate the reporter's personal presence at a news event. But you must judge for yourself the authority of the person who is the source of a given news story. Is he qualified to say this? Does he possess enough information to make such a judgement?

Perhaps even worse than the named news source who has no authority to make a statement is the unnamed source. This individual appears frequently in news of national or international politics. Some facts cannot be announced officially, but when a reporter uncovers them – he reports them as rumour, without naming his source. He may make no reference to a source, or he may state that his information comes from an 'informed source, or a 'usually reliable source'.

## 4. Slanted News

A newspaper may present news in a biased or 'slanted' way, either accidentally or intentionally. You, as a newspaper reader, are likely to misunderstand the true facts of a slanted news story. All the facts may not be there, or may be so presented that their relative importance is not clear to you.

A slanted news story may get written intentionally or unintentionally. In the limited time before a deadline, the reporter may not have time to gather all the facts, he does his best but he may miss an important part of the story. An informant who furnishes the reporter with news may not know all the facts, or he may deliberately lie about some of them, but the reporter may not find this out. If the reporter has a strong personal opinion about his subject, he may deliberately or unconsciously allow his opinion to creep into the story. He may do this by what he writes, by his choice of words suggesting favourable or unfavourable meanings, by emphasising certain facts, or by omitting other facts.

News may also be slanted by the way stories are arranged on a newspaper page, or by the way a story is emphasised. A news item of major importance may be hidden on a back page, while sensational but unimportant stories fill the front page. Important stories may sometimes be left out entirely.

Slanted news is not always the fault of the reporter. Frequently, it is the editor or publisher who directs that a certain policy be promoted in the paper. Slanted news challenges your alertness and your ability to think clearly about what you read.

## 5. Beware of appeals to your emotions

Propaganda is the name given to any organised attempt to influence your thinking or your actions. It may be good or bad. There is no objection to such propaganda as 'Join the Red Cross!' 'Donate blood.' 'Vote.' This kind of propaganda, expressed in slogans, news stories, or editorials, is usually constructive and worthwhile.

Nearly, all advertising material is propaganda. It is an attempt to persuade you to buy. Good advertisement is generally honest and straightforward in its presentation and repetition to convince you. But the propaganda to watch for is the kind that tries to mislead you.

Propagandists appeal to your emotions in many ways. Half-truths are common. "Doctors recommend this toothpaste." How many doctors? Who are they? And why do they recommend it? These questions may remain unanswered. Or another: "This mouthwash proved best by extensive tests." Best for what? Who conducted the tests? What kind of tests? With what other brands of mouthwash was it compared?

Other propagandists want you to do something because "everybody is doing it". "Follow the crowd!" It suggests. "Everyone's voting for this candidate." Or a testimonial is offered: "Famous movie star Aamir Khan chews this brand of bubble gum." This implies that you should select this brand because Aamir Khan is famous and wealthy, and in this way you will share something with him.

Use of misleading names or titles is another common means of spreading harmful propaganda.

All these devices appeal to your emotions rather than to your common sense. It is easier to relax and be fooled than considering carefully what you hear and read. This is why propaganda often succeeds. You don't bother to think statements through, and as a result, you don't recognise propaganda when you see or hear it. Therein lies the greatest danger as also the greatest challenge of today's high-speed modes of communication.

□□□

# News Gathering

## What is News?

*Shyam Varma passed an English test today.*

*Satish Varma was nominated for 'Outstanding Achievement Award' today.*

One of the above items is news for a local newspaper. The other is not. Why? The successful reporter develops a 'nose for news'. He knows what his readers want, and how earnestly they want it. If he were to analyse why some happenings are news, while others are not, he would tell you:

"People are news. These people must be doing something. And what they are doing must interest the newspaper reader."

This gives the formula:

### People + Action + Reader Interest = News

The two examples at the beginning of this chapter now begin to make sense. There is a person in each, and there is an action in each. But the second sentence is newsworthy because the magnitude of the event is more than the first one.

Readers' interest is the result of certain specific news elements. These elements are as follows:

## 1. Nearness

- *A loud explosion severely damaged the Telephone Exchange building yesterday.*

- *A loud explosion severely damaged a building in Afghanistan.*

Which news item is more interesting to the readers of a local newspaper?

An event that takes place nearby is of more interest to readers than something occurring far away. Daily newspapers tell of many happenings in their own area that would be of no interest to readers in another city. To the local newspaper reader, most events taking place within the community are of greater interest.

## 2. Timeliness

- *Mrs. Sonia Gandhi is to visit Darjeeling next month.*
- *Mrs. Sonia Gandhi is to arrive in Darjeeling tomorrow.*
- *Mrs. Sonia Gandhi arrived in Darjeeling yesterday.*

Which two of these sentences are more interesting?

The closer a news is at the time of a newspaper's publication, the more timely, opportune and more interesting it becomes.

## 3. Importance

- *My father left for Kolkata yesterday.*
- *The President of the United States will attend the special session of the Parliament today.*
- *A change in University graduation requirements affecting one student was announced today.*
- *A change in University graduation requirements affecting two thousand students was announced today.*

One sentence in each pair has considerable news value. The other does not. Why?

The news element 'importance' might also be called prominence, size or consequence. The 'bigness' of anything is one of the main factors in generating reader interest. A daily newspaper will generally develop more reader interest with a story about a fire gutting a building worth crores of rupees than a fire resulting in damage of a mere hundreds of rupees.

## 4. Names

- *An unidentified person was found shot dead in a hotel room today.*

- *Jacob D'souza, CEO Megamix Industries, was found shot dead in a hotel room today.*

You may not know Mr. Jacob. But a number of people know him, however, and there is always a chance that you might be familiar with Mr. Jacob. People will read a news story with names in it because they are interested in seeing their own names or the names of friends or relatives in print. They will even search through long, boring lists trying to find a familiar name. Judicious use of names makes many stories of past events, which otherwise have lost their timeliness, worth printing in a newspaper.

## 5. Conflict

- *Subash Sthapit is the only candidate running for election to the office of the Chairman of the Municipality.*

- *Sailesh Pradhan, Raju Biswas and Asif Iqbal have filed nominations for election to the office of Municipal Chairman.*

This news element makes the most of dramatic situations. Mystery, suspense as well as conflict may be inherently present to add to its mass appeal. Elections, contests, discussions and arguments are interesting to readers because of opposing forces, frequently leading to drama and suspense. The sports stories are most sought after news in a daily because there is conflict and suspense involved in any game. Court trials create drama because of the clash between conflicting forces.

## 6. Variety

- *An explosion in the market place left several injured.*

- *An explosion in the market place blew a two-year-old into pieces and left three adults severely wounded.*

Any event that is new, strange, original and has never happened before, or is not likely to happen again develops readers' interest.

## 7. Human interest

- *Local nurses completed three-week training in childcare.*

- *A ten-year-old in college? Students were amazed to see Rahul Rawat, a ten-year-old kid, walking into Room 306. He stormed out of the school after completing his 10+2 in two months with 98 per cent aggregate.*

True, the second example is written in a more interesting way but it also contains a news element called human interest, which has to do with events in human life. Sadness, happiness, talent, achievement and success characterise human interest in the same way that these are a part of living. The activities of children often create human interest. Animal stories have similar appeal for many readers.

## 8. Examples for unusual incidents

- *High level of violence, arson, bomb blasts has been planned during the polls...*

**Beacon[17], Jan 15, 1998**

- *Steven Spielberg, the famous film director of Jurassic Park fame, has related his horror at discovering that he was the target of a homosexual stalker who planned to kidnap, torture and rape him.*

**Beacon, Jan 15, 1998**

Funny or unusual incidents appeal to newspaper readers. Clever, positive or astounding people always attract the readers.

## Traits a Good Reporter must have

A 'Reporter' is the most important person in the news-business. All news, whether intended for newspaper, magazine, radio or television, must be collected by someone. The person who does this job is the

---

[17] http://www.beacononline.wordpress.com

reporter. As long as there is a free press that is privileged to publish or broadcast facts, reporters will be needed to gather those facts.

Who are these men and women who perform the never-ending task of collecting bits of news and fitting them together into interesting paragraphs for the readers, listeners or viewers? They have become reporters in various ways. Many of them are college graduates; many have had wide experience in other fields of work. Some of the younger ones have been trained in college/schools of journalism; some have been writers, teachers, or salesmen. Some started without formal training, by going to work for a small newspaper and learning journalism the 'hard way'.

Although their backgrounds may differ greatly, all successful reporters have certain qualities in common. These traits and habits are equally important for the success of a reporter. Willing young people can develop requisite traits and skill-sets over a period of time to become successful reporters.

- A good reporter is interested in his job. To him, the thrill of putting together a good news story and the daily roar of the newspaper press are always exciting. He goes beyond what is required of him and is always striving to improve his work.

- A good reporter does not have to be told what to do. He thinks of new ways to approach the same old news. He accepts assignments willingly, and carries them out well. He is always searching for other news ideas, and when he finds one, he develops it into a good story.

- A good reporter keeps looking for the facts until he has found them. He is careful not to offend or antagonise people, but he keeps searching and asking until he has his story.

- A good reporter enjoys meeting and talking to everyone. He is the kind of individual in whom people put faith and confidence. Newspapermen thus get many unsolicited stories or tips.

- A good reporter is always curious. He wants to know what people are doing and why. At the same time, he respects their right to privacy, unless they have put their lives into the 'public domain' by words or actions.

- A good reporter wants to be fair. He realises that there always exist two sides to controversial questions and he tries to present both.

- A good reporter knows that he has a responsibility to print the truth. He never takes things for granted because if he does, he may find that he is reporting personal opinion rather than facts.

- A good reporter has learnt to communicate an idea in correct and effective English. He writes in simple, direct prose without using complicated sentences. At times, his writing is lively and interesting.

- A good reporter has an insatiable desire for facts and has learnt how to put seemingly unrelated bits of news together into an informative and well-organised story.

- A good reporter has knowledge of many fields. He reads a great deal about people and what they have done, and his curiosity keeps him interested in all kinds of current events.

- A good reporter has learnt what news is, and what the readers of his newspaper expect from him, and he always tries to meet those expectations.

## Locating News

There are four main ways of locating news:

1. Many reporters for newspapers have definite beats or 'runs'. There are people or places where they regularly go in search of news. A beat may include, for example, the local police station. A reporter covers his beat as the first step in finding news stories. He is expected to contact each source of news, he is expected to write it in proper form, regardless of how important it may seem to him, or reports it to the editor, who will assign the story to another reporter.

2. The editor makes assignments of reporters for every important news event. An assignment usually includes the catch line or

title of the story, the name of the person to see, the time when the story is due, the number of words to be written, and in general what the story should contain. Assignment ideas come from many sources.

3. When a reporter learns that something is going to happen, or hears about something that has just happened, he uses this tip as a starting point and he tries to find more information about the event. A tip differs from a beat in the sense that it represents news that is probably not related to any of the news events previously known to the editorial staff. (It may, of course, then become the subject of an assignment.) A reporter who is alert and keeps his eyes and ears open will hear about many news events that would not ordinarily reach the paper through beats or assignments.

4. It is sometimes possible to invent a news story. Of course, you can't make up a news story about an event that didn't happen, much as you might wish to! But there are certain kinds of stories waiting for an imaginative reporter to think of.

## Interviewing for a News Story

### Interview 1

| Reporter1 | : | Uh… you don't have any news this week, do you? |
| News source | : | No. |
| Reporter1 | : | Well, thank you. |

### Interview 2

| Reporter 2 | : | Good morning. I would like to talk to you about the conference. |
| News source | : | What would you like to know? |
| Reporter 2 | : | What is it all about? |
| News source | : | Well, it's about problems being faced by the local labour union. |

72

**Interview 3**

**Reproduced from Beacon, Feb. 15, 1998 issue**

| | | |
|---|---|---|
| Editor | : | Sir, what are you trying to emphasize by the word Revolutionary Marxist? |
| Mr. R. B. Rai | : | The Communist Party of India – Marxist (CPI – M) has lost its revolutionary character and has become entangled with rigidity. Marxism-Leninism will never die until it is dynamic and changes with time. The CPI – M says that the foreign capital is the main enemy of socialism, yet they are inviting them to do business in the state. |
| | | We are not against foreign capital, things should change with time and politics should be pragmatic. |
| Editor | : | You talked about consensus candidate. What do you mean by that? |
| Mr. R. B. Rai | : | The votes in the Darjeeling hills must not be divided. If any party offers to give us firm commitment to our four main election issues, we could contest the election with mutual support. |
| Editor | : | Your main issue is creation of a separate state. If you win, how do you plan to work for it? |
| Mr. R. B. Rai | : | The platform for separate state has already been there, we will work both collectively and individually for the state in Delhi by raising the constitutional implications in a democratic manner... |

Which interview will be most likely to appear in print?

Newspaper reporters get most of their news, not by waiting for it, but by going out, meeting people. This is the heart of reporting – the most fascinating and interesting part of newspaper work. The reporter talks to people who are 'in the know' about different events. He asks questions to be sure he understands. When he is finished, he has the pleasure of being on the 'inside' of knowing what's going to happen, often before many of the people who are directly affected come to know about it.

Some reporters are fortunate enough to be eyewitnesses to the events they are covering – for example, the story about a speech or the report of what takes place at a meeting. They can write their stories from personal experience. But most reporting – and this includes all future events – is done by getting the facts from one or more people who know them. This is interviewing, which will be dealt with here. (The problems of eyewitness reporting accounts will be covered in a later chapter).

Most people are eager to have a newspaper that tells about what they are doing. However, they frequently need help in determining what will be news to the newspaper reader. In interviewing for a news story, you must plan ahead as carefully as possible. Only a thorough preparation for an interview will result in a well-written, complete, and interesting story.

## What to do before the interview?

First of all, know whom you are to see. If you have an assignment, know what the story is about. Then be sure to think carefully about the subject of your interview.

### 1.  If you have an assignment

Find out as much about the story as you can from the editor or other staff members, from recent issues of the newspaper, or from other sources.

- Is this an event which takes place annually? Find out what happened last year. The similarities will help in your reporting, and the changes, which have the most news value, will be clearer by comparison.

- Is this event similar to other events, which take place from time to time? Familiarise yourself with the way they have been handled in your newspaper.

- Is the subject unfamiliar to you? Read about it in your library, using books, magazines, encyclopaedias, dictionaries, or other sources of information. If you are assigned to cover a story about a seminar on numismatics, and you don't know that 'numismatics' means 'coin collecting', you would not only seem stupid to your news source, but you probably would also come away with a poor news story, or none at all.

**2.  If you are covering a beat**

Find out from previous issues of your paper what type of story usually originates from this beat.

- If it is a group that meets regularly, when did it last meet? What happened then? Were there hints as to what may have happened since then, or what may happen in the future?

- If it is a person, such as the Municipal Chairman, what type of news usually originates from this source? Have there been any hints in recent issues of the paper, or in your conversation with politicians or intellectuals as to what sort of news you might find?

- After getting these things clear in your mind, write out the questions you will use as guide in securing the information you want. Be prepared to ask other questions as the interview progresses so that you fully understand the information you receive.

## What to do during the interview?

1.  Contact the person who is your news source. If he is a politician, you can call his party office and get an appointment. State that you are a reporter and ask when it would be most convenient to interview him. Perhaps, it will be at once. If so, go ahead. If not, make a definite appointment.

2.  Carry a small pad of paper and a few pens with you, so that you can take notes on all facts, dates, and names of persons or places.

3. Check the spelling of all names. Copy any direct quotes that you think you would like to have printed exactly and ask him whether you can quote him. If you confine yourself to writing down important facts in abbreviated form, your news source will not mind waiting while you do it. He is personally interested in having these facts correct.

4. In interviewing your news source, be pleasant and courteous. Remember that he is a busy person, but also that he is interested in correct and complete coverage of his news story. Don't worry if he doesn't follow your prepared questions exactly, ask other questions to be sure you understand fully, and to draw him out on what you consider to be important points.

5. At the conclusion of the interview, check your notes with your source, and thank him. Politeness is a good public relations technique for your newspaper and yourself.

## What to do after the interview?

Write your news story immediately, while the interview is still fresh in your mind and while your scribbled notes mean something to you. In case, a new query crops up in your mind, return to your news source for an answer. Don't make it a habit, though. It's a sign that you did not try to understand fully during the interview.

If time and conditions permit, it is good to take your finished story back to your news source to be checked for accuracy of facts. But don't expect help in writing the story. Organising the information and using correct form is your job.

## Finding Background Information

In preparing to interview your news source, and again while writing your news story, you frequently need information from stories that have either previously appeared in your newspaper, or check facts from other sources.

Leading daily newspapers often maintain elaborate libraries for use of their reporters. The newspaper library is called the morgue, since one of its most common uses is obtaining information for obituary stories. A clipping of every story ever printed about a famous person would go into the file picked from newspapers, magazines, and other sources: pictures, family information, and so on. The existence of a morgue explains how a newspaper printed only a few hours after the death of a famous person can contain whole pages about his life.

Large newspaper morgues contain clipping files on other subjects of current interest. There are encyclopaedias and up-to-date reference books, as well as current news magazines and other newspapers.

There is, of course, a complete file of all issues of the reporter's own newspaper. Modern libraries use microfilm to avoid bulky storage of old newspapers. In this process, a small picture of each page is made on a roll of film. It is possible to locate a particular page of a certain issue rapidly, and then read it easily with a special viewer.

The current trend in newspaper writing is to interpret news. Rather than just learning what happened, the newspaper reader wants to be told why it happened. The reporter preparing a story about a proposed tax increase must comment on what the tax rate has been in previous years, what the rates are in other cities, what experts feel is a fair tax rate, and what competing newspapers have said about the proposal. He can find all this information in a well-equipped morgue.

Small newspapers can rarely afford to keep up an extensive morgue. They are likely to have only a file of back issues of the paper. For other facts, they rely on the storehouse of information in the editor's mind and on the public library.

You should be able to find some of the following aids to good reporting in the staff room of your newspaper:

- Complete files of your newspaper for past years
- Clipping files on selected important topics
- Supplementary textbooks on journalism, advertising, photography or printing

- Dictionary – the most recent editions

- Dictionary of synonyms (Thesaurus).

There is one important thing to remember about the morgue and the other references available to you – they are worthless to you unless you use them often!

□□□

# The News Lead

## The Lead

The first paragraph of a news story is called the lead (pronounced 'leed'). To summarise an entire news event in 25 or 30 words is not easy. Hence, the ability to write good leads is probably the most important single skill you will learn in your study of journalism.

Carefully examine the following story from *The Telegraph*. Notice how the lead gives a summary of the most important facts.

### Civic Chief cracks whip as garbage grows

*Calcutta: The civic authorities have set up a "task force" and an "action line" to clean the garbage piled up on city streets in the wake of "mass absence" of sweepers over the past few days.*

*Confronted with overflowing garbage vats, unswept roads and choked gutters, officials of the Calcutta Municipal Corporation (CMC) decided to force the issue on Thursday. They urged citizens to call them directly if they had complaints regarding garbage management in their neighbourhood.*

*At an emergency meeting, Commissioner Alok Burman said complaints received on any of the dedicated action line telephone numbers – 244-6015, 244-2365, 244-2748 and 244-7064 will be addressed "within two hours of their automatic registration".*

*"They (the citizens) must give us details of the name of affected area, the exact location of the offering garbage vats and the present method of its disposal.*

*I promise that their complaints will be sorted out in two hours flat," announced Burman.*

The news is presented in a special way. What are the reasons for this kind of writing in a newspaper?

- It answers your questions at once: When you think of news, you want to know immediately, "What happened? Who did it? Why or how, when and where?" You don't wish to wade through limitless paragraphs to learn these things. The news story, putting the important facts first, answers your questions in the order you want them answered.

- You can decide which stories to read: Few people read all of a newspaper. Remember different types of news are intended to appeal to different readers with varied interests.

- It helps the busy reader: The reader, who has only a few minutes but wants to know what is going on in the world, can get a complete summary of the day's news by reading only headlines and lead paragraphs.

- It helps the reporter write his story: Writing a summary first, then detailing facts in order of importance, is the natural way of thinking about a news event. It is easier for a reporter to write this way.

- It meets the cut off test: In the busy, rushed routine of a newspaper office, the copy reader or editor does not have time to rewrite a story if it is too long. He simply crosses out the last few paragraphs, containing the least important facts. A well-written story can be cut at the end of any paragraph back to the first, and it will still tell you essentially what happened.

## Building the Lead

The lead is the heart of the news story. An interesting and carefully planned lead will attract readers to your story. A flat, uninteresting lead will drive your readers away. Building a lead which appeals to your readers and which summarises the story in 25 or 30 words take practice. Follow the steps below, one at a time, to succeed in this difficult task.

## Find the 5 W's and 1 H

The first step in building a good lead is to find the answers to six single word questions:

### WHO?

Who did it? Who is involved in the event or fact?

### WHAT?

What happened? What did someone do?

### WHEN?

When did it happen? When will it take place?

### WHERE?

Where did it happen? Where will it take place?

### WHY?

Why did this event happen? What was the reason for it?

### HOW?

How did it happen? By what method was it accomplished?

If you answer these six questions, choosing the most important answer to each one, you have the material for a satisfactory lead.

Now that you are familiar with the 5 W's and 1 H questions, apply them to an actual story. When you, as a reporter, interview a news source, you take notes that include all the facts of the story. From these notes, you must develop your lead.

Check your notes carefully. Decide which important facts answer each of the questions. List the 5 W's and 1 H questions down the left hand side of a piece of scratch paper. Opposite each question, write the facts that answer it.

Now look over your list, starting with WHAT. If you have written more than one answer here, decide which statement is important as the backbone of the story and which statements are merely details. Cross out the unnecessary details, leaving the principal fact to answer the WHAT question.

Go over other five questions, crossing out the facts that are not directly related to the information answering your WHAT question. Probably you will now have only one answer to each question. However, WHO might include several names even if all are not of equal importance. It is also possible that there will be more than one answer remaining to the WHY or HOW questions in some cases. Decide which facts go into the lead.

As you work with these activities, it will probably occur to you that not all six questions need to be answered in the lead. You are correct. Some of the answers are really not that important. Good news leads rarely include the answers to all six. However, remember only after you have discovered and listed these, you are in a position to decide whether you should leave some of the answers out. To take a shortcut and use only those answers which you find easily is to risk leaving an essential part of your story out of the lead. Consider the following points as you write your leads:

WHO: The name of a person who has done something noteworthy is essential. On the other hand, your WHO may be the sub-inspector or a social worker. These names are not often important enough to be in the lead. They should be used later in your story. If you have many important names, you may wish to say in your lead "Eight Congressmen won..." and put the actual names in the second paragraph.

WHAT: You do not have a news story unless something happened. WHAT will generally always be present.

WHEN: The time or date is needed for events that happen at a specific time, whether past or future. It is unnecessary in stories about general announcements or about plans that are under way. WHEN is rarely important enough to belong at the beginning of your lead, except in special cases, it should be put at the end of the paragraph.

82

WHERE: The location of a news event is often understood to be the local community. If this is the case, leave it out. Your reader doesn't care whether the Planters' Club meeting was in room 12 or room 318. WHERE can be omitted from stories of past events unless the place is directly involved in the story. On the other hand, WHERE is very important in future events, such as dances or meetings which your reader may wish to attend. Your WHERE belongs at the end of the lead with the WHEN.

WHY and HOW depend on the story and you will have to consider each one carefully. Neither, either, or both may be essential. Usually one is important and the other is not. A story with an important WHY factor is unlikely to have an important HOW and vice-versa.

REMEMBER: You can safely discard one or more of these six major facts only after you have traced and considered all of them.

After making an excellent beginning towards preparing a good lead, when you have selected the answers to the 5 W's and 1 H questions, and having picked the really essential facts from among these answers, the next step is the selection of the key feature that is most important or most interesting.

The key feature may be the answer to any of the 5 W's or 1 H questions.

**Put the Key Feature First**

Examine the following first lines of news stories.

| *Would you read these?* | *Or, these?* |
|---|---|
| • On the morning of…. | Steven Spielberg, the famous film director… |
| • There will be a meeting… | Famous television show host Shekhar Suman… |
| • Preparations are under way... | High level of violence, arson, bomb blasts…. |

In the second group, the reporter finds the key thought and emphasises it at the beginning of his story. The result is a lively lead that will make its readers want to find out more details.

The first line of a news story contains only five or six words, but among these words you must include some that contain enough 'spark' to make your readers want to go further into the story. Your lead is the showcase for your story, and you begin it with the most interesting material you have.

These examples show how 5 W's and 1 H elements may be featured:

*WHO?*

C. R. Natarajulu, a freedom fighter, was honoured to mark the golden anniversary of Indian Independence.

*WHAT?*

Rasika Ranjani Sabha will stage a play on September 17.

*WHY?*

To assist in the implementation of the project, the representatives of Ford will visit the Darjeeling Red Cross.

*HOW?*

Six people were killed and two others injured when the roof of a house collapsed in Kotrahalli in Karnataka on Wednesday.

*WHEN?*

On September 13, there will be a music recital by Palladam Venkataraman Rao and party.

*WHERE?*

The Mylapore Fine Arts Club, Oliver Road, Mylapore will hold concerts by senior musicians.

To bring the key thought of a news story to the lead and to state it in striking words, you have a wide choice of sentence construction.

Different kinds of sentences or different parts of speech are suited to emphasising various elements in your lead. One can use any of the following ways:

1.  Begin with a noun.
2.  Begin with a quotation.

84

3.  Begin with a question.

4.  Begin with a striking statement.

Placement of the key thought in its proper position at the start of each lead provides the main reason for using a variety of lead beginnings. A secondary purpose is to furnish more interesting reading.

Suppose each story on your front-page begins in the same way:

- A committee of the trade union will meet today.

- A football game will be played on Saturday.

- A dance attracted many students last night.

Not very interesting reading, is it? Because of the similarity in the beginnings of these leads, they all seem dull. Your readers would skip over some stories if all were written this way.

Regarding selection of starting words for leads, it is important to remember that articles are generally rather weak words. Try to avoid the articles 'A', 'AN', or 'THE' at the beginning of your story whenever possible. They say little to your reader. However, if it seems impossible to keep your key thought at the beginning of the lead without an article, use it!

Do not begin your story with 'THERE' (there is, there was, there will be, etc). These words say absolutely nothing. Instead, change your sentence construction by using strong, lively words:

**Poor:** There will be ten gifts for early birds who join the course.

**Improved:** Gifts will be given to ten early birds joining the course.

Try to avoid using the word 'HELD' as the main verb in your sentences. Find a substitute when possible:

**Poor:** A meeting of the Trade Union members will be held today.

**Improved:** Trade Union members will meet today.

Perhaps you have noticed that some leads became complicated and burdensome as you tried to make them complete. Too many words were required to say everything. You needed to furnish a complete

85

summary of the story. This was especially true when you tried to include all of the 5 W's and 1 H facts and even after you left out the non-essential material for later paragraphs of your story.

Brief, direct, simple sentences are best for news stories. They are easier to read and more likely to be understood. Notice how the following one-sentence leads are improved by dividing the ideas into two sentences:

**Complicated:**

Nearly 250 business honours students have each purchased Rs. 20 tickets permitting them to attend the Annual Business Fair and to participate in different events associated with the fair.

**Simple:**

Nearly 250 business honours students will take part in the Annual Business Fair. All have purchased Rs. 20 tickets permitting them to attend the fair and participate in its different events.

There will be times, of course, when a single short sentence summarises your story better than two sentences. However, division into two, or even three short sentences can improve most leads containing more than 20 words. To check if your lead is complete and clear, give it the following tests:

- Does it read smoothly? Read the lead aloud. If you run out of breath, it is too long. Thirty words (five lines of fonts) are enough. Shorten it by leaving out unimportant words or ideas. Or divide it into two or even three sentences. Read it aloud again. Do all the words fit together into an understandable pattern? Does it make sense?

- Does it contain all necessary facts? Check again for the 5 W's and 1 H facts from your notes. Have you included all necessary facts in your lead, and left unimportant details for later paragraphs?

- Is the key thought first in the lead? Look at the first five words in your lead. They should include the key thought and they should be live, sparkling words that say something.

- Will your lead attract readers? Look again at your notes to make sure you have used the most interesting fact, the 'WOW!' element, in your lead. If you have done so, and if your lead is written in an interesting way, there is an excellent chance that you have succeeded in what you have tried to do.

Your reader will not only read your lead paragraph but will continue on to the end of the story.

▢▢▢

# Putting the Story Together

## The Inverted Pyramid

The Inverted Pyramid is a method of putting a story together. Here the top-heavy look is intentional the arrangement puts the big facts first and the little details last. Take the following story for example. Note how each fact has more news value than the one following it.

### Crash fear hangs over London hit parade

*London, April 20: Organisers of a $2 million Indian film awards ceremony here say they are finding it difficult to charter a single aircraft to fly 300 of the biggest names in Bollywood to Britain because of fears that "the entire industry would be wiped out" if an accident occurs.*

*"These things do happen," said Mambo Sharma, whose company, Wizcraft International Entertainment, will stage the event inside Skyspace adjacent the Millennium Dome on June 24.*

*"It happened with Manchester United," he said, referring to the air crash in Feb. 1958, in which seven of the top footballers of Manchester United died in Munich.*

*Amitabh Bachchan and Yukta Mookhey will release details of the International Indian Film Award (IIFA) at a press conference at the Dome on April 25.*

*The reigning Miss World will be one of the comperes on the big night. Her co-host might be Shah Rukh Khan.*

*Sharma, who is known in the business as "Mambo", has spent weeks in Bombay, finalising an event intended to place Bollywood on par with Hollywood. Negotiations are also on to rope in some stars from Hollywood for the ceremony.*

*"In terms of annual turnover estimated to be $200 million, we are the second biggest film industry in the world and the highest for the number of films made," Sharma said.*

*The list of names, Sharma is approaching includes Dustin Hoffman, Jeff Goldblum, Richard Gere, Robert de Niro, Sylvester Stallone and Will Smith. He will be lucky if any of them is willing, and indeed free to come.*

*The exercise will not be cheap either.*

**(Reproduced from The Telegraph)**

The reason for writing a news story this way is that the reader finds the information he wants more readily and understands it better. The reporter himself thinks more logically while preparing it; and the editor may adjust its length to the space requirements because it meets the cut-off test. The first paragraphs after the lead contain essential details and the last paragraphs of the story may be eliminated if there is no space for them.

## The Chronological Story

Occasionally you will find it more suitable to write the body of your story in chronological order, stating the facts in the order of their occurrence. Each event connected with each other is presented in the order in which it will take place. This order bears no relation to the importance of the event. The first two paragraphs are needed to summarise and connect activities.

## The Composite Story

A composite news story combines two or more news events because these events have a connecting reason or theme. It is a story with more than one key thought.

The body of a composite news story may be arranged in several ways, all varieties of the inverted pyramid or the chronological order story. But the simplest way is to treat each event as a separate story. Following a lead refers to all events and thereafter mentions the next, and so on. The events may be arranged in chronological order or in the order of their news value; the latter plan is more common.

□□□

# Writing in Newspaper Style

Following points should be kept in mind while writing in newspaper style:

1. Start sentences with key thoughts.

2. Keep your sentences simple.

3. Use simple words with clear meanings.

4. State each idea in a few words.

5. Use nouns as modifiers to shorten sentences and state facts directly. News in English often uses a noun as a modifying word. This process eliminates many prepositional phrases, which slow up reading.

6. Use colourful words. Certain topics lend themselves readily to the use of colourful words. Descriptive or action stories are especially adaptable, but all your stories will be improved if your sentences draw word pictures.

7. Use verbs for description.

8. Personalise your news. People make news. To report news effectively, you must tell about the people responsible for it. Use names in your stories wherever you can. Names sell newspapers. Names are what readers want in their news.

9. Distinguish between fact and opinion.

10. Never editorialise a news story. Newspaper editors state their opinions in editorials. From this name comes the term editorialising,

the practice of expressing a reporter's opinion in a news story. The newspaper reader does not want to be bothered with what the reporter thinks about news event, he wants to know what happened. If he wishes an opinion, he will turn to the editorial page for thoughtful comment by an expert who is paid to analyse and criticise. The editor's opinion is far more valuable to the reader than that of the reporter.

Also such editorialising is fairly easy for the reader to detect, and for the reporter to avoid.

11. State the opinion of news sources.

12. State your facts accurately.

13. Tell the whole truth.

14. While choosing the right words, never use first or second person pronouns. The presence of one of these pronouns suggests that the reporter may have drifted into editorialising. Their effect is to bring the writer's or reader's personality into the story. Use pronouns properly.

15. Be careful to state the time correctly. 'When did it happen' is a very important question.

16. Names must be spelled correctly.

17. And most important of all, think critically while writing a news story.

□□□

# Covering News

While covering news, it is important that one should keep the following things in mind:

1. Keeps news stories of past events short.

2. Emphasise the 'Why' angle.

3. Project the future while reporting the past.

4. Use as many different names as you can.

5. Reach all your news sources. For one thing, you must develop a smooth working system for collecting and covering news.

## Making a Meeting Report Interesting

A story that tests your skill in deciding what is important and what is not is generally the report of a meeting, for example, the meeting of a political party or the legislature. Many things may be discussed and voted upon in such meetings. You must use your discretion and decide which of these have news value and which are mere details.

The mechanics of writing an interesting 'meeting' story are simple. First, attend the meeting personally and make your own notes. Second, select the event or decision that affects the largest number of people or that seems most interesting and important. This is your key thought and hence must be featured in your lead. Third, give all the facts concerning paragraphs of the story in the order of their importance, leaving the least important to the last.

# Covering a Speech

There will be times when you will be assigned to write a story about an assembly or meeting, featuring a speaker. Reporting a speech accurately is difficult. You must sift among the many words spoken, find the essential facts, and then present these facts in an interesting way. A speech story is in a way similar to an interview story, for you must show the personality of the speaker and indicate how his audience receives him.

Following points are to be noted:

1. **Obtain Background Information**: Interview the people close to the speaker to get the speaker's name and topic. Inquire about the purpose of the speech. Obtain biographical data about the speaker from your news source or the library, or your own newspaper if time permits, read about the topic in reference books. This would be especially desirable if you are faced with a technical or unfamiliar subject. On rare occasions, you may be able to obtain an advance copy of the speech to be delivered. Review this in preparation, but attend the meeting in any case for the speaker may not present it exactly as planned.

2. **Listen for the Main Idea.**

3. **Copy Two or Three Interesting Quotations.**

4. **Interview the Speaker if Possible**: You can learn more about the speaker's personality if an opportunity arises to interview him briefly, before or after the speech. Ask a few questions about his experiences or his principal ideas in the speech. Any understanding you gain will help you write a clear story.

5. **Begin the Lead with a Direct Quotation.**

6. **Briefly identify the speaker and occasion**: A sentence or phrase in the lead or second paragraph is adequate for this purpose. Tell who he is, when he spoke, and to whom. Then go on with your report of what he said. Other biographical information

can be reflected in your summary of his talk or left for the final paragraphs.

7.  **Vary your manner of presentation**: Mix paragraphs of direct quotation, indirect quotation, and summary. One problem is to avoid repetition of "He said". The use of synonyms or other terms suggesting this meaning can accomplish this.

                                                                    □□□

# Colourful News Features

## Features

A feature is anything in a newspaper that is not straight news or advertising. Features are like the 'icing' on the cake. If well chosen and well written, they add variety to any newspaper. Most features are based on news events in some way. In fact, the editorial staff in a newspaper uses the word 'feature' to identify a news feature, which tells of human-interest items, presents entertaining news, or explains and interprets facts. Other types of feature are related to news. They include editorials, host columns, personality interviews, fashions, editorial cartoons, and movie and television reviews. Successful newspapers include non-news features but limit them. Some of these features are book reviews, crossword puzzles, comics, and cartoons. Almost any topic that would interest or entertain readers is an appropriate feature subject.

## Identifying and Writing News Features

News features may be identified in three ways. First, they report news events, although the news content is not as important as the way the stories are written. Second, they are written informally, with extensive use of descriptive verbs and entertaining phrases. Their leads are designed to attract readers rather than to recite essential facts. They may have surprise endings. And third, they may be printed on news pages or on the editorial page.

The reporter who finds and writes news features must be a keen observer.

## Entertaining News Features

News features may be divided generally into two categories – those that entertain and those that inform. The entertaining news feature appeals to the emotions of your readers. Since the news value is slight, the way these stories are written becomes vital to their success.

Subject for entertaining news features are everywhere. You often uncover them on your beat or while following out a routine news assignment. What would be dull facts if presented in straight news form, come to life when you develop them imaginatively into a news feature.

Alertness, observation and luck may help you find the best of human-interest features. Watch for unusual happenings, offbeat situations, sayings that make you laugh, or clever ways of doing things. Consider the humour all around you on the local scene; it forms the foundation for many news features. Daily newspapers often publish features about sad or touching subjects, but remember that readers prefer the lively, humorous kind.

Things to be kept in mind while writing entertaining news features:

1. Get all the facts.

2. Determine your approach. Consider your material. How will you handle your facts? How will you portray the people involved? Will you build up to a climax or surprise ending?

3. Write your lead – the lead does not have to tell all essential facts, but it must include the most eye-catching information, attract readers, and tell your readers what kind of story to expect.

4. Tell your story in the best possible way.

5. Use imagination and colour. Here is your opportunity to unleash action verbs and descriptive words that must be restrained in ordinary news writing.

6. And, above all, stick to the facts.

## News Features that Inform

Many outstanding news features are written to inform readers, rather than to entertain them. These are careful, thorough studies of particular situations, classes, or activities.

To write an informative news feature, you must follow the same steps as you do for an entertaining one. Here, again, your lead is important.

□□□

# Describing a Personality

Following points should be kept in mind while writing a personality story:

1.  Make plans for your interview. Find out as much as you can about the individual you are to interview. Use directories, the newspaper morgue, or the library. Talk with people who know him.

2.  Prepare for the interview. Make an appointment with the person you are to interview. Check your personal appearance. Neatness will help you create a good impression as you meet your subject. Carry two or three pens and a small pad of paper. Make brief notes on facts and main issues (ideas) and put down the exact words of any statements you may wish to quote.

3.  Enjoy your interview. Be pleasant and courteous. Begin the interview by getting acquainted. And above all, relax and enjoy the conversation.

4.  Notice how he looks. Study his face, his smile, his expressions, his clothes, the way he moves his hands or eyes.

5.  Put the story on paper at once, while impressions are fresh in your mind. An interview story falls easily into the inverted pyramid pattern, although some of the less formal techniques suggested for news features may fit the kind of story you are preparing.

Your lead should identify the person, and feature an important fact or quotation relative to the 'tie in' or the main topic of your interview.

□□□

# The Art of Making Columns

A column is a feature printed regularly in a newspaper. It usually appears on the same page in every issue and has the same title over a period of time. The author's name is given in a by-line when the same person writes it regularly.

Good columns have several characteristics:

- The subject appeals to many readers.

- The writer, usually an authority in his field, is capable of finding fresh material for each issue and presenting it in a lively manner.

- The column has an original title which defines its content or purpose. Some daily newspapers, knowing that the author's reputation will attract many readers, use only his name as a headline for the column. Others have an arresting title, often incorporating the columnist's name. Many columns are syndicated and sold to newspapers across the nation.

While almost any topic of interest to many readers may be considered of sufficient merit for a regular column, several questions should be considered before valuable space is reserved, issue after issue:

1. Does it have wide appeal?
2. Can it be kept interesting?
3. Do the authors have unusual reporting and writing ability?
4. Will it appear regularly?

5. Will the title be eye-catching?

6. Will it have an unusual appearance?

Choose suitable columns for your newspaper such as:

**Letters to the Editor**: Your readers furnish the ideas; even write most of this column. Their letters asking for information, commending certain actions, or suggesting improvements, make a popular column. The reporter in-charge selects letters that have wide appeal, and prepares brief answers if the letters require a reply.

*Sydney Morning Herald's 'Opinions and Letters Page'*

*Austrian newspaper De Standaard's 'Special Interests' Page*

The reporter in charge of choosing which 'Letters to the Editor' are to appear in print should apply certain principles when making his selections. He should look for letters which are more than one paragraph in length, on the assumption that such presentations might be more thorough, more tactful and hence, more constructive. He should look for letters in which opinion is backed by facts and in which there is a fair consideration of more than one side of a question. Finally, he should choose letters which present new and interesting information on the subject involved, rather than those which belabour one small point in a heated, emotional manner.

**Hobbies or Special Interests**: Columns about albums, television programmes, fashions, cars, or hobbies, written by someone who is well informed in a particular field, appeal to reader interests. Of these, columns about albums or music are most common. They owe their appeal to the popularity of various songs or musicians.

**Humour**: A column, using original material, is excellent if cleverly done and terrible if poorly done! It takes a special kind of writer to succeed. Unless you have such an individual on your staff, your paper is better off without an attempt at original humour.

**Use Names but avoid Gossip**: The newspaper that prints gossips faces several difficulties:

- Lack of effort and imagination gets demonstrated. It is easier for reporters to repeat rumours than to dig out interesting news items.

- One small group is usually featured. There is a strong tendency to write about the same few persons week after week.

- There is a danger of libel. If a half-truth is printed, or a truth, which damages someone's reputation, is leaked in the paper, the reporter, the newspaper, and the publisher may find themselves in a serious trouble.

□□□

# Planning an Editorial Page

An editorial page can be exciting, different and attractive. But success doesnot just happen. The entire page must be organised in advance.

As a rule, an editorial page contains no advertisement. In six or eight page papers, the facing page often contains more feature material. If so, both pages must be planned together. In daily newspapers that carry more than 20 pages, the location of the editorial page may vary, but it is generally fixed and is the same in any given newspaper. Major city papers use the facing page for related feature material.

The main goal of an editorial page is to furnish the reader with background information about the news of the day. Editorials serve this purpose by interpreting or explaining current events. Editorial cartoons, columns, news features, personality sketches, or letters to the editor are planned to contribute to a better understanding of current happenings.

## Collect Suitable Material for an Editorial Page

The newspaper's masthead identifies your editorial page. Many kinds of articles may be chosen to complete the page. Some of these are not appropriate for use anywhere else in the paper.

There are numerous kinds of copy that are appropriate for an editorial page. These are:

- **Editorials:** The entire page exists as a showcase for your editorials. They are chosen and written with care, and are the central attraction of your page.

- **Editorial Cartoons:** When well conceived and illustrated, editorial cartoons share the spotlight with your editorials and can influence your readers in the same manner.

JOURNALISM IS THE FOUNDATION OF A DEMOCRATIC
SOCIETY

PROTECT IT !
CHERISH IT !
STRENGTHEN IT !

*An Editorial Cartoon*
*(© Beacon April 1998)*

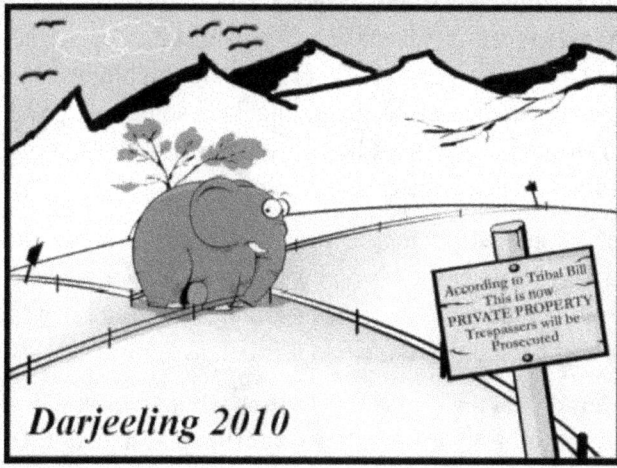

- **News Features:** News features are the most useful stories in your newspaper. They are equally at home on news page, sports page, or editorial page. Their variety in subject, approach, length and style gives them high reader appeal on the editorial page.

  Both entertaining and information news features should be used regularly.

- **Personalities:** Interview or personality stories attract interest on your editorial page.

- **Letters to the editor:** This feature is particularly appropriate for the editorials, and needs the same careful preparation.

- **Columns:** Other columns of all kinds are desirable editorial page material.

- **Views on the News:** Interpretation of news includes giving background information, presenting sidelights on news events, showing how several events are related, and providing editorial comment.

  Unpleasant as the thought may be, many of your readers have only a passing acquaintance with the world around them. Their knowledge is limited to headlines that catch their eyes as they open a newspaper to the comic page, or to radio or TV news highlights. Your paper can perform a real service by giving them some background about news of the week. In addition to top world and national news, important local events can be interpreted.

  A news commentary may appear as a regular column, or a single topic may be discussed in a news feature. A good reporter who is a prolific reader of current books, magazines, and newspapers is your best choice to handle this difficult assignment.

- **Reviews:** Reviews may be written about movies, books, art exhibits, plays, musical productions and other forms of entertainment.

  Critical thinking makes a review different from a news story or news feature. In order to make judicious comments and treat the subject matter distinctly, the reviewer must have a wide-ranging experience to compare his subject with other successful or unsuccessful productions and present valuable comments to the reader. He must know something about the skills required for success in the art form he is describing or the book he is reviewing. Major city newspapers pay music, book and art critics extremely well because of their extensive knowledge about their fields.

A review should be brief but thorough. Meaningful comments about your topic may be included. Unimportant ideas should be left out. When considering a current book or movie, write your review in a way that encourages reading of the book or viewing of the movie if it is worthwhile.

- **Creative Writing:** The editorial page offers possibilities for occasional input of original creative literary efforts. Individuals, who prepare them, may not be staff members, because a different kind of literary ability is required for it.

The following areas offer excellent possibilities:

- o Short-story (keep them under 250 words)
- o Unusual personal experiences, perhaps with a surprise ending
- o Short essays on topics of human interest
- o Humorous tales or experiences
- o Poems

## Assembling the Material into an Effective Editorial Page

In selecting material for an editorial page, keep all of the following points in mind:

- **Variety in form and content:** Mix several kinds of material, such as news features, columns, reviews etc.,

- **Contrast in appearance and approach:** You need a mixture of humorous and serious articles, stories of different lengths, and writing in various styles. Do not overlook the appeal of photographs, cartoons, and drawings.

- **Relation to news:** The best editorial page material has definite news 'peg'. Too many articles unrelated to current events make a dull page. A good plan is to spotlight three or four items related to the same major news event: an editorial, a cartoon, and a news feature, perhaps a letter to the editor. Each approaches the event in a different way, adding to an understanding of its background.

However, do not tie every article on the page to one event; this will look contrived and artificial, and only weaken the page.

- **Reader interest:** Keep in mind that the individual articles, as well as the appearance of the whole page must appeal to your readers.

- **Page makeup:** As you plan the page, remember to allow space for your newspaper's masthead. Traditionally, this listing of the newspaper's name, policies, and staff members has been placed at the head of the editorial column. However, the modern trend is to move it to the bottom corner of the page so that more important reading matter may be featured at the top.

**Austrian newspaper**
*De Standaard's* **Editorial Page**

*Hindustan Times'*
**Editorial Page**

□□□

# Editorials – Voice of the Newspaper

The editorial is the voice of the newspaper. An editorial seeks to encourage critical thinking, to mould opinion, and to promote action. If the newspaper performs its duties well and says whatever it has to on crucial issues with logic, purpose and enough force, it can influence public opinion and make people take action.

Even when the results are not outstanding, thought-provoking editorials are valuable because they stimulate discussion, planning and action.

The power and influence of daily newspaper editorials is even greater than those of the weekly newspapers. Thousands of people vote for a particular candidate in a national election because the newspaper recommends him. By persuading its readers to take action, a newspaper can promote all kinds of improvement and development activities in the regions of its circulation. On the other hand, a newspaper that is indifferent or destructive in its editorial policy can do untold damage to the community.

Editorials appear at two places in a newspaper. The traditional position is on the editorial page, in the left-hand column under the paper's masthead. Modern composition of page often places the masthead at the bottom of the page, and editorials, too may be moved from their traditional position. When an editorial is considered to be of sufficient importance, it may be placed on the front page of the newspaper. In this case, it would be labelled 'Editorial' and would probably be enclosed in a box.

Since editorials reflect a newspaper's policy on local or national affairs, important ones are written by the editor himself, or by editorial writers under his instructions. Editorials by other staff members may also find place on this important page.

Editorials are generally printed in larger type and in a wider column than other material on the editorial page. There may be either one editorial or a full column of editorials in each issue of the paper. Sometimes the column includes editorial paragraphs, which are short, pertinent, even humorous comments on current events.

Editorials are rarely signed. They should not be confused with daily columns, which express opinions of well-known writers and which always have a by-line giving the writer's name. Occasionally, when the topic is of utmost importance, the front page editorial is signed by the editor or the publisher.

## Types of Editorial

There are four types of editorials: (i) Editorials that interpret, (ii) Editorials that criticise, (iii) Editorials that persuade, and (iv) Editorials that praise.

**Editorials that Interpret:** These may give further information about a news event. They may explain or interpret an important happening in a way that is not possible in news columns. Many daily newspaper editorials are of this type. While opinions or comments about the news event may be included, they do not form a major part of this kind of editorial.

**Editorials that Criticise:** These editorials are pegged to a current news topic or situation, and are critical of actions, standards or problems. To be constructive, criticism must be positive rather than negative. It should praise good traits and features and motivate further development by pinpointing all that is bad, lacking or anomalous. Editorials bearing criticism have little value unless a solution is suggested.

**Editorials that Persuade:** These are the 'top salesmen' of the editorial world. Their basic purpose is to inspire or force someone, perhaps the reader or an official body, do something. They differ from the critical editorial, which may suggest a solution as it comments on a problem, in that the editorial writer has already decided his solution is convincing. He now uses his writing powers to 'sell' you this solution.

**Editorials that Praise:** A worthwhile project for an editorial column is to praise, congratulate, or commend people and organisations that have done something well. A feeling of goodwill results for such an editorial.

## Writing an Editorial

Following points should be kept in mind while writing an editorial:

**1. Select a Topic:** Your study of daily newspaper editorials should have convinced you that only topics with a current news angle deserve editorial space. The best editorial subjects are those of current interest to the readers. These topics make your writing easier, too. It is not easy although it can be done – to convince your readers of something.

You can write editorials about general topics such as morality, ideology and so forth. Unless these are major issues for you, such editorials will not be widely read. These subjects are hard to present adequately without preaching. When so much is happening around you, it is not hard to find good editorial topics. From these you can prepare editorials that will be read, thought about and acted upon.

**2. Collect all the Facts:** Daily newspaper editorial writers may do seven or eight hours of research for each hour spent in actual writing. They leave no stone unturned in their search for facts and arguments. If this is true of professional writers, then you, as an amateur can hardly be justified in hammering out an editorial during the last 20 minutes before deadline. Your readers will recognise your hasty writing and leave it unread.

Perhaps you cannot follow a professional's schedule because of various reasons. But you owe it to yourself, to your paper and to your readers to do a thorough job of obtaining all the pertinent facts before you begin writing.

If you have chosen your topic wisely, your editorial will be based on a news event. Some reporter has covered the event and written stories for your newspaper. You should begin with the facts in these stories. Ask the reporter for any additional facts he may have omitted from his stories.

Next, plan your research programme. What sources, written or personal must be sought out to get a complete picture? An editorial writer must be more than an organizer of facts and a good salesman. He must be a penetrating reporter as well. He must dig deeper and try harder to understand reasons behind a news event than the reporter who is writing a news story.

Suppose you are assigned an editorial about a coming election and your town is where election is not taken seriously, your task is to convince your readers to vote. How can you do this?

- Begin with the news stories assembled for your paper. Don't fail to get the facts collected by a reporter or reporters for stories in the forthcoming issue, in which your editorial is to appear. Talk to the reporter to find out his feeling about the election, to collect any unpublished facts, and to learn his news sources. You will save time if you do not have to repeat this individual's work, especially if he has done it well.

- Now that you have some facts, consider what additional information you need.

- Find out the arguments for and against voting. Arguments against voting may come from various sections of society. Some may say elections won't change anything; some may feel it's a waste of time and money. Even though you are trying to convince people to vote, don't overlook the arguments against it. Answering them may be strong salesmanship.

- Talk to voters and get their opinions.

- Check your facts and figures again. You won't use them all, but if you don't understand, your editorial may lack a valuable argument. Go to all the news sources necessary to get additional facts. The actual writing of the editorial is not difficult if your groundwork has been well done.

**3. Make Every Word Count:** An editorial is an essay. This allows more freedom in the use of words, sentences and paragraphs than a news story, in which the reporter faces limitations of form and space. For example, you may use more adjectives or different types of sentences, if they serve your purpose better. It takes your finest writing to 'sell' an editorial idea. Anything less than your best will not 'make the sale'.

And always be brief, exact and avoid the first person pronouns in editorials, just as you do in news stories.

**4. Make Your Reader Think:** The only way your editorial will achieve its goal is by stimulating each reader to do some constructive thinking for himself on the discussed issue. Hours of deliberation by your editorial staff will prove worthless unless, by the sheer power of your words on the editorial page, you 'start the wheels rolling' inside each reader's head.

Involve your reader's personality. However, be careful not to destroy your reader's confidence by preaching to him.

**5. Write a Headline that Forces the Reader to read it:** An editorial does not have the same kind of headline as a news story. It has only one purpose: to attract readers and to persuade them to read the editorial.

Depending on your newspaper style, you may add more latitude in writing an editorial title than in headlining a news story. A typical form is a single line across the wide editorial column. Frequently, the editorial title is in a different style of type from other headlines.

## Editorial Cartoons

Editorial cartoons are powerful weapons used by many dailies and weeklies. Drawn about controversial topics, they promote much public discussion. In the past, newspapers considered them so important that they placed them on the editorial page and were usually related to the leading editorial. A few cartoonists have earned nation-wide fame and their work appears in newspapers from coast to coast.

While it is not likely that editorial cartoons in a small town newspaper will exert so much influence, they will attract the eyes of almost every reader. Readers will react constructively if cartoons are planned and presented in a positive manner.

*© Beacon Online 2008 Barun Roy - Source*
*http://www.beacononline.wordpress.com*

Good editorial cartoons are not hard to produce. If you are fortunate enough to have a staff cartoonist, put him to work. Even if you have no staff cartoonist, there is a way to get cartoons. Somewhere on your staff or in the neighbourhood there is an individual who can draw cartoon figures. Your editorial board or editorial page staff can plan cartoon ideas related to editorial topics or to current events and assign them to the artist. This combination of artist-plus-journalist usually produces meaningful editorial cartoons.

## Crusading for a Cause

Editorial crusades or campaigns are the outgrowth of a creative editorial policy which seeks to do something and not merely to act as a mirror of town/city life. The paper seeks to lead reader opinion.

What is involved in a successful editorial campaign? The answer is quite simple. Confidence and hard work are the pre-requisites needed to form public opinion to the extent that it garners the machinery for accomplishing the targeted results. This requires unrelenting effort and imagination. Proper timing is necessary as is the fact to keep the burning and revived in every one's memory until your goal is reached.

An editorial campaign is a combination of all possible efforts to influence public opinion. News stories and pictures are combined with editorial cartoons, and features, over a period of several issues. In addition, a full-scale campaign calls for posters, talks, meetings, petitions, and other devices.

114

Crusading requires cooperation and help from the local administration. Before you start, discuss your plans with your publisher. Maintain close contact with him as you proceed. Be sure you understand exactly how your campaign fits into the general programme of your publisher.

Consider the problem and your assets before embarking on a crusade. Unless you are willing to devote space on consequent issues for prolonged time, issue after issue do not plan a campaign. You may feel there are better ways to channel your energies and allot your newspaper space. But if your project is worth acting upon, plan your crusade carefully.

Before you begin, contact those people in the town/city who will be affected, to determine whether your proposal is feasible. Eventually you will gain enough support for your campaign so that you will not be working single-handedly.

□□□

# Presenting Sports Action

All types of news stories and features may be written on sports topics. Each item is prepared according to standards for its particular style.

Time is an essential consideration for the sports page and the weekly or fortnightly newspaper is at a definite disadvantage in this respect. Ordinarily you must leave detailed game summaries to daily newspapers. You have little reason to write "blow-by-blow" descriptions of sports events, unless your paper has space for detailed summaries in addition to advances and features.

Argentinean newspaper *Olé's* Sports Page portrays the importance of sports in Argentinean life.

Short game summaries are practical in most papers. Many advantages are available to sports writers: they often have more personal knowledge of the team and its coaches than reporters of daily newspapers, more time to write and more opportunity to develop interpretative sidelights.

Writing at your leisure rather than under deadline pressure a few hours after the game, you can explain many 'WHY' and 'HOW' questions that usually you are not able to. WHY the team played in an unusual way? WHY a particular athlete didn't seem to be exerting his best?

HOW the critical play that won the game was planned? Interpretative reporting can be excellent when deadlines are not imminent, when time is available for reflective thinking and when interviews can be arranged with coaches and players after they have rested.

Good accounts of games are written as a result of eyewitness reporting. In this sense, they are similar to reports of speeches or meetings. You observe carefully, taking notes on spectacular action. If the scorekeeper's records are available to you, you may depend on these for basic facts but you must add colourful highlights gained by personal observation. If these records are not available, you must keep the necessary records yourself, and at the same time watch for outstanding plays. Post-game interviews with players, coaches and officials will add to your understanding of the event. From all these facts and impressions, you will select appropriate items to feature in your story. In most papers, you will not be allowed much space, and you must make every word convey something important.

## Review or Summary

Summary stories, giving results of several games or reviewing a complete season may serve several purposes:

- To review and highlight the activities of an entire season

- To summarise the events in a major sport when space cannot be allocated for reports on individual games

Sports summaries need not be routine recitations of scores and dull facts. Use the names of outstanding players. Briefly but vividly describe the highlights of the game.

If you try to be 'fair' by writing one short sentence about each game, you will have a dull pattern of sentences monotonously reporting the same idea, and no one will want to read your story.

Typical sports pages do not have space enough for all possible advance, report and summary stories. Thus, you should avoid repetition and still make an effort to give your reader the total picture of one sport.

## Features

Do you want your sports page to keep your readers informed and entertained? If yes, use features! Almost any kind of feature is suitable.

Entertaining and informative news features will liven up the page. Seasonal summaries are best if treated as informative news features. Interpretative stories about new rules, sports history, styles of play or game backgrounds add interest. Humorous incidents are always worth space for the attention they attract.

A sports personality or 'Player of the Week' story outlines a star player's accomplishments, describes his interests, activities and ambitions. Coaches and physical instructors also make fine subjects for personality sketches.

To add life to your pages, try:

- Quizzes on present or past sports events
- Summaries of little-known facts about sports
- Statistics on team effort or individual player's records
- Prediction contests, with subscription or gifts as prizes

Editorials on athletic topics are usually of interest to readers. However, the informality of the sports page suggests that comment is more effective when given the personal touch possible only in columns or by-lined stories.

## Write your sports story informally but correctly

Some sports reporters feel that the informal style of a sports page permits sloppy writing. Nothing could be farther from truth. Only those who have mastered the techniques of formal composition can do successful informal writing. When this has been accomplished, you have a basis for stretching these standards into an informal style. Without this training, your attempts at informality may end up as poor writing.

Good sports writing follows the standards for news writing that you have learned in previous chapters and have applied in writing news stories. The following points deserve special comment:

1. A good sports lead is complete and concise.
2. Use colourful but not trite expressions.
3. Use the correct names of the players.
4. Keep the time element in mind.
5. Use box scores properly.
6. Interpret the facts if you are qualified to do so.

## Plan an Interesting Sports Page

Sports space in your paper should be allotted in proportion to other news, features and advertising, taking into consideration the amount of interest in sports that your readers have. Typically, sports news appears on the last page, sometimes the third, of a four-page-paper. Advertisements usually fill part of the page, posing a problem to the sports editor. In four-page papers, advertising is divided between the sports page and the second news page. A reasonable amount of space is left for sports news.

Some papers keep approximately the same amount of advertising on the sports page day after day, varying the

*Sports page of Hindustan Times*

second news page according to the total volume of advertising. When the paper has six or more pages, the sports display can be improved by

*Sports page of the Times of India*

leaving the sports page, as well as the editorial and front pages, free of advertising. An alternate plan, more pleasing to your advertisers, is to allow two facing inside pages for sports and printing advertisements on both pages.

As you plan sports page, keep in mind that sports are vigorous and fast moving. A page that reflects this vitality and speed is possible if you consider several points.

- Plan stories and photographs well in advance. Make assignments to reporters according to your sports events schedule, bearing the time element in mind.

- Arrange for various kinds of material on the page: advance stories, reports, photographs, features and columns.

- Cover all sports, major and minor, according to the reader interest. Brief stories on minor topics take up little space, make the page attractive, add to reader interest by publicising different names, and appeal to different groups of readers.

- Feature advance stories rather than reports of past events.

□□□

# Copyreading and Proofreading for Accuracy

A story having news value must undergo some changes if it is to appear in print. Who is responsible for correcting it?

To begin with, every reporter copy reads his own stories because he is expected to submit them in correct form. A copy without errors is called a 'clean' copy. Any successful reporter's copy is consistently clean; it only requires few changes. But not all reporters have the same experience, information or skill. Therefore, a newspaper must have a specialist to see that the written material is accurate and clear. In smaller newspapers, the copyreader may be one of the editors. In most papers, a person whose only job is to read and correct copy does this work.

A copyreader's job is important due to following reasons:

- Truth needs to be entured. Accuracy, while not easy to attain in the rush of newspaper deadlines, is a major objective of every newspaper.

- To present news in direct and readable style, which includes improving the lead and the organisation of the story.

- To check on spelling, punctuation, and sentence structure; to see that copy conforms to the newspaper's writing style; and to make sure that the reporter's ideas are conveyed in such a way that the reader will understand them.

- To 'boil down' stories to a length commensurate with their actual news value.

- To remove any elements of bad taste, to avoid libel and to eliminate editorialising.

- To mark typographical specifications for the printer.

The copyreader usually writes headlines as well, although this may be a work of a headline specialist. On daily newspaper (1) each reporter may prepare headlines for his own stories, in which case the copyreader would revise them, if necessary; (2) the copyreader may write them; or (3) page editors may do this work as they place stories on their pages. This last method is probably the most practical. Page editors evaluate each story in relation to others on the page, and indicate its importance by placement and the type of head it is given. This also makes for greater variety in headlines.

When a story leaves the copydesk, it is in final form for publication and no further changes should be necessary. Various editors may make corrections as they fit, but responsibility for thorough checking is the copyreader's not the editor's.

## Copyreader at Work

The copyreader is not a mere mechanical checker of words and sentences. To do this job adequately, he must possess a large fund of information and knowledge. For example, he must know the names of people around and their positions to make sure that names are properly spelled and titles correctly used in copy. The copyreader must have a general knowledge of local organisations, policies, programmes and history. Many times a reporter's innocent error of fact is caught and corrected by an alert copyreader who remembers how the event was handled the previous year.

# Copyreader's Marks

1. L or $\pi$ or $\llcorner$          Paragraph

2. No $\pi$          No Paragraph

3. Write $^{or}$ check he $^{a}$ dlines          Insert letter or word

4. (MD)          Spell out
   Medicinae Doctor          Abbreviate
   twelve          Change to figure

5. worke          Delete letter
   Working          Delete letter and join
            separated elements.

   write a good story          Delete word and join
            separated elements.

6. Benzine          Close up space.

7. Stet          Leave as originally written.

8. In the building.         
   Twelve students.......          Set in one unbroken line, or
            join separated matter.

9. go/home          Insert space

10. |John Johnson, director|          Transpose elements
    working          Transpose letters

11. Des moines          Change to capital
             letters

12. John Johnson, Director          Change to lower
             case letter

13. Folo copy          Set copy as it is written

14. ] [          Indent both sides of text
             centre matter is column

15. (x) or ⊙          Emphasizes period so that
             printer won't overlook it

16. In the house          set boldface

| 17. <u>college</u> | set italics |
| 18. <u>Des Moines</u> | Set smallcaps, same size as lower case letters. |
| 19. (more) | copy continued on next page. |
| 20. ⓺ or # | End of story |

21. If you cannot find a mark that fits your need, use any simple mark that you feel sure will tell the printer (or DTP operator) what you want him to know.

He must have a clear understanding of English usage. He must correct spellings, sentence structure, punctuation, capitalisation, and all other errors to meet the standards specified in the newspaper's style sheet. He must be alert to common writing errors that hide or distort the reporter's meaning.

Tools of the copyreader include a good recent dictionary, a thesaurus for synonyms, a writer's handbook or English grammar textbook, copies of the headlines schedule and style sheet and a local telephone directory.

In copyreading, you must find the mistake and correct it so that the copy reads smoothly. This is why reporters submit double-space or triple-space typed copy (or write handwritten copy on every other line) and leave extra space at the top of each page.

A universal system of editing by way of copyreader's marks has been developed (see Copyreader's Marks). When properly used, the marks are clear to editors and printers alike. They save hours of rewriting or copying. Every reporter learns these marks to save time in preparing his stories, and also to understand completed news copy. Copyreaders must use marks so that typesetters (or DTP operators) understand exactly what is expected of them.

Notice how copyreader's marks have been used in the following example:

The students of st. Joseph's College took a field trip to the local tea factory in Darjeeling the jayshree tea estate on Nov. (fifth) to learn about the processing of tea.

The copyreader has much to keep in mind as he reads a story. Copyreading is more effective if you consider problems one at a time. Only an experienced copyreader can recognise and deal with every type of mistake in one reading of a story.

When you copyread, go over your story several times, looking for different types of error each time. Take them in order of the following steps:

1.  Make sure every statement is accurate.

2.  Make sure your story is well organized.

3.  Eliminate one-third to one-half of its words.

4.  Eliminate editorialising, evidences of poor taste, and libellous statements.

5.  Make sure your meaning is clear.

6.  See that your copy agrees with style sheet rules.

The copyreader makes certain that all copy follows the rules of his newspaper's style sheet, which outlines the desired punctuation, capitalisation and spelling. This step clears the meaning, for these grammatical rules are also intended to improve communication between reporter and reader. Paragraphs are also easier to read if the same types of word are always capitalised, if titles are always presented in the same form, or if other matters of style are handled uniformly.

7. Retype the story, if necessary.

8. Mark typographical specifications: Every newspaper has one standard column width and one regular style of body type. Your DTP operator or page designer sets all copy to these specifications unless it is clearly marked for different treatment.

9. Headline the story.

## Proofreading

Proofreading, which takes place later in the publication schedule, is the process of comparing 'printed' material against the original copy, to find any possible errors made in transcribing it. Proofreading is quite different from copyreading. The copyreader is the last person who makes changes in a reporter's story. While when you are proofreading, your only task is to see that the proof checks with the copy.

The form in which proofs come to you will differ somewhat according to the kind of publication process used by your newspaper. In the case of printed papers (letterpress) or offset newspapers using typeset copy, the proofs appear as single columns of type printed on long strips of paper. For mimeographed papers, the typed stencil serves as the proof; for offset papers prepared with a computer, the finished job of typing must be proofread. While the method of marking for the last two newspapers is different from that used with a printed proof, the importance of accurate proof reading is equally acute, and the proof is identical.

Correcting a reporter's mistakes at the time of proofreading is difficult and wastes time that you cannot spare. If your paper is commercially printed, you pay extra attention to these corrections. Of course, if you do find an error that cannot be allowed to pass, you must correct it.

Proofreading is usually done by a team of two, a copyholder and a proofreader. The copyholder reads aloud from the copy, indicating paragraphs, commas, and other punctuation and spelling out proper names. The proofreader follows on the proof, marking corrections.

## Proofreader's Marks

Though Proofreaders' Marks are universal, they do at times offer slight alterations based on countries, papers and above all the habits of the proofreaders.

Here are some examples of Marks.

| INSTRUCTION | TEXT MARK | MARGINAL MARK |
|---|---|---|
| INSERT TEXT | be or to be | /to/not |
| REPLACE TEXT | to be or not the be | /to |
| DELETE TEXT | it's a a beautiful day | ℘ |
| DELETE TEXT | he's a simple boy | ℘ |
| DELETE/CLOSE SPACE | it's a beaautiful day | ℘ |
| LEAVE UNCHANGED | he was not in error | STET |
| INSERT PERIOD | to me The point is | ⊙ |
| INSERT COMMA | red white and blue | ⊙ |
| INSERT COLON | three groups the | ⊙ |
| INSERT SEMI-COLON | he said she said | ⊹ |
| INSERT APOSTROPHE | its a beautiful day | ⌄ |
| INSERT QUOTATIONS | Wow! she said | ⌄/⌄ |
| INSERT SINGLE QUOTES | Wow! she said | ⌄/⌄ |
| INSERT PARENTHESES | it was the time of | ⦅ / ⦆ |
| INSERT BRACKETS | it was the time of | ⟦ / ⟧ |
| INSERT ELLIPSIS | And so it goes | ⊙⊙⊙ |
| INSERT LEADERS | 1999 Wine List | ⊙⊙⊙ |
| MAKE BOLD ITALIC | he was not in error | bf + ital |
| MAKE ROMAN | he was not in error | rom |
| MAKE LIGHT FACE | he was not in error | lf |
| CAPITALIZE | Sam kennedy said | cap |
| MAKE SMALL CAPS | he lived in 300 B.C. | sc |
| CAP & SMALL CAP | julius caesar | cap + sc |
| MAKE LOWER CASE | SAm Kennedy said | lc |

| | | |
|---|---|---|
| MAKE LOWER CASE | Sam KENNEDY said | (lc) |
| SUPERIOR | E=MC2 | ² or (sup) |
| INFERIOR | comprised of H2O | ₂ or (sub) |
| NEW PARAGRAPH | to me. The point is | ¶ |
| RUN ON (NO NEW PARAGRAPH) | to me. The point is | no ¶ |
| MOVE TO NEXT LINE | she could not re- | (runover) |
| MOVE UP FROM NEXT LINE | she could not re- cover from it | (move up) |
| WRONG FONT | that beautiful day | (wf) |
| TRANSPOSE LETTER | he was not in error | (tr) |
| TRANSPOSE WORD | he not was in error | (tr) |
| MOVE TEXT | He tried to call her immediately | (tr) |
| CENTER TEXT | ]The End[ | (center) |
| INDENT TEXT | ]In the beginning | (indent) |
| NO INDENTATION | In the beginning | (flush) |
| MOVE TEXT RIGHT | 1999 Financial Plan] | ] |
| MOVE TEXT LEFT | [1999 Financial Plan | [ |
| LOWER TEXT | She has a big heart | ⌊⌋ |
| RAISE TEXT | She has a big heart | ⌈⌉ |
| ALIGN TEXT/COL. VERTICALLY | ‖to me and the others. The point is that | ‖ |
| ALIGN HORIZONTALLY | She has a big heart | (align) |
| ADD SPACE | She has a bigheart | # |
| CLOSE UP SPACE | She has a big h eart | ◡ |
| SPELL OUT | She weighed 20 (lbs) | (sp) |
| INSERT EM DASH | Space the final frontier | $\frac{1}{m}$ |
| INSERT EN DASH | during 1996 1999 | $\frac{1}{n}$ |
| INSERT LEADING | He tried to call her but she was not home | (#) |
| DECREASE LEADING | He tried to call her but she was not home | (reduce #) |
| REMOVE UNWANTED | but she was not home | (x) |
| ADD RULE | The Big Chill | 2 pt rule |

# Miscellaneous Marks

## Style of Type

(wf) Wrong font (size or style of type)

(lc) lower case letter

(lc) Set in LOWER CASE

C capital letter

(Caps) SET IN capitals

(c→lc) Set in lower case with INITIAL CAPITALS

(sc) SET IN small CAPITALS

(c+sc) SET IN Small Capitals with initial capitals

(rom) Set in roman type

(ital) Set in italic type

(ital caps) SET IN ITALIC capitals

(lf) Set in lightface type

(bf) Set in boldface type

(bf caps) Set in boldface CAPITALS

⊽ Superior letter ⊽

⋏ Inferior figure ⋏

## Position

⌐ Move to left

(ctr) ⌐ Center ⌐

⊔ Lower letters or words

⊓ Raise letters or words

= Straighten type (horizontally)

‖ Align type (vertically)

(tr) Transpose

(tr) Transpose (order letters of or words)

## Spacing

(ld in) Insert lead (space) between lines

(td ld) Take out lead

⌣ Close up: take out space

♯ Close up partly: leave some space

## Equalize space between words

(Eq #) Equalize space between words

## Insertion and Deletion

the/? Caret (insert marginal addition)

ℐ Delete (take it out)

e Correct letter or word marked

(stet) Let it stand (all matter above dots)

## Paragraphing

¶ Begin a paragraph

(no ¶) No paragraph

(run in) Run in or run on

(flush) No indention

## Punctuation (use caret in text to show point of insertion)

⊙ Insert period

⋏ Insert comma

⊙ Insert colon

;/ Insert semicolon

⌣/⌣ Insert quotation marks

⌄ Insert apostrophe

(set) ? Insert question mark

! Insert exclamation point

=/ Insert hyphen

—/m̄ Insert one-em dash

(/) Insert parentheses

[/] Insert brackets

## Miscellaneous

⊗ Replace broken or imperfect type

⊘ Reverse (upside down type)

(sp) Spell out (twenty lb)

(au) /? Query to author

(Ed) /? Query to editor

⌐ Mark off or break, start new line

□□□

# Headlining a Story

What do you see first when you look at a newspaper? Headlines, of course! But not all headlines attract your attention equally. Which of the following headlines would make you want to read the story it publishes?

**Trinamul Congress cadre shot dead**

**President Clinton to face impeachment**

The job of a headline is to summarise and highlight its story. Even if you never read another word of a newspaper, you will get much information from its headlines.

- Headlines help you decide which news stories you will read and which you will not. Headlines must highlight its contents in such a way that it makes a story interesting and enhances your curiosity to read more of it.

- You are furnished with a brief summary of each story. A busy reader, looking only at headlines, should get a fairly complete picture of the news of the day.

- You can also decide from the headline size how important each story is. The largest or most bold headlines are on top of the stories that the editors feel have most news values.

- You get a good idea from the size and style of its headlines, as to whether this newspaper is conservative or sensational in its approach.

Each news story is told three times – in the headline, in the lead and in the body of the story. Of these, the shortest and hardest to write is the headline, yet it is the most important.

## Who writes Headlines

In many daily papers, this is the copyreader's job. After checking a story for accuracy, form, and style, he prepares a suitable headline according to the editor's directions. However, some large city papers employ headline writers. Small newspapers may assign various people to the task. Copyreaders or headline writers bear this responsibility. Sometimes when a reporter is assigned a story, he is told the kind of headline it requires, and he is expected to write it. But generally a 'page editor' whose duty is to plan, arrange, and follow up production of a page does the job.

## How to Write a Headline

Writing headlines is like writing telegrams. You must make every word count. If you had to pay 50 paise a word, you wouldn't waste your money on words like 'the' or 'a' or 'there are' or on unnecessary adjectives. Headlines are limited in the same way. You must tell your story in two or three lines, and each line can contain just so many letters and spaces.

You do not prepare your headline before you write your story. The reporter staring at a blank piece of paper asking, "What can I say in the headline for a story I'm going to write?" is doing his job backwards. Write your story first, taking special care of the lead. If your lead is well written, you can then use it as a basis for your headline.

The points which should be kept in mind while writing a headline are as follows:

1. Select key words in the lead.
2. Write a short telegraphic sentence using the key words.
3. Divide your sentence into two or three lines.
4. Use the correct verb form.
5. Learn the standards for headline writing.

As you have seen, headlines use language in special ways. You have already studied the following principles:

- Put the story's main feature in the headline. Take your facts from the lead.

- Make every headline a complete sentence, with a subject and a verb.

- Omit 'is' and 'are' from headlines wherever possible.

- Use the present tense to indicate current and past happenings.

- Use the infinitive wherever possible to indicate future happenings.

- Use the active voice of the verb, rather than the passive.

- Do not use the articles 'a', 'an' or 'the'.

- Do not divide words, proper names, verb phrases, propositional phrases, or closely related adjective-noun combinations from one line to the next.

- Do not begin a headline with a verb.

- Do not use abbreviations, except for renowned organisations such as BCCI, LIC, GIC etc. When initials are used, do not allow space or add periods (.) between letters.

- Use numbers only if they are important. Avoid starting a headline with a number. However, this practice is less objectionable than the use of a passive verb or an awkward headline.

- Use single quotation marks.

For example, **Lok Sabha to pass the 'women' bill today**

6. Make your headline vital.

7. Learn to use your headline schedule: No paper can operate successfully without a headline schedule. This is a printed sample of various available headline patterns, indicating typefaces and the unit count per column of each in the type sizes or fonts available, and assigning a number to each. By using this number,

the headline writers, editors, copyreaders and printers all 'speak the same language'. The planning of a headline schedule requires considerable study by the editor, the adviser and the printer.

Your headline schedule will include basic news headlines, almost always following the flush left pattern. Some of these will be for single column stories and some for two or three-column 'spreads'. There will be occasional banner headlines, which extend across the full page. Most newspapers also employ a few headlines with 'kickers' above the main headline. To add variety, there may be different fonts for one or two unusual headlines or features. And, if your newspaper uses two-deck headlines there will also be fonts for these.

**Flush-left or No-count Headlines**: Caps and lower case letters make the basic headlines easily readable in modern newspapers. For good appearance, each line must fill at least three-quarters of its column; it may extend across the entire column if desired. Flush-left headlines may be used in various widths and sizes of type, to suit each story's importance or placement on the page:

1. **Single-column Heads** (two or three lines)

2. **Spreads Headlines**: Headlines extending across two or more columns are common in newspapers. They add variety and improve the appearance of a page, and may have one or two lines.

### TIGERS SET FRIDAY DEADLINE

**Left leader**

**son burnt**        **BOOKSHOPS JUST**

**in Tripura**        **A CLICK AWAY**

3. **Banner or Streamer Headlines**: An important story may merit a banner head across the top of the front page or the sports page. Since this headline extends across all the columns, it must be written to an exact unit count.

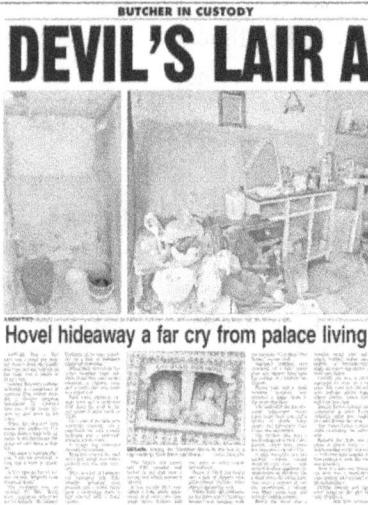

BUTCHER IN CUSTODY

DEVIL'S LAIR A    SQUALID HUT

Hovel hideaway a far cry from palace living

4. **Kickers**: Modern informal typography allows the use of 'kickers'. These are short lines above the main headline, basically used to highlight or introduce the headline.

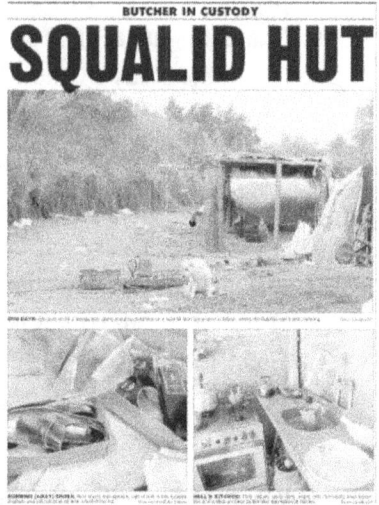

BUTCHER IN CUSTODY

DEVIL'S LAIR

In the above example, a kicker 'Butcher in Custody' is given to introduce the headline 'Devil's Lair'

Several points should be noted when it comes to kickers:

- It is in smaller lighter type than the main headline.

- It is usually underlined.

- It is frequently followed by a dash or a series of dots.

- It is sometimes like a complete sentence, with subject and verb but this may not necessarily be so.

- It never repeats words used in the main headline.

- It may begin a thought that continues into the main line. In this case it is called a "read – in".

A kicker is particularly or peculiarly suited to introduce a column or a regular feature. The kicker states the column's title, and the main line introduces an appealing idea from the copy.

**Novelty or Feature Headlines:** Features demand unusual headlines to attract attention and to brighten up your pages. You will use them especially on human-interest news features. Various kinds of kicker arrangement, partial or full boxes around headlines, or other off beat devices, announce to your reader: "Here is something different you'll want to read!"

**SHOULD HE DIE?**
WEIGHING SADDAM'S FATE: PAGE 5

**Subheads:** Long stories give a 'grey' appearance to a news page. This adverseness may be corrected by inserting subheads between paragraphs. Subheads are one-line boldface headlines, usually in the same size type as the body of the story. They may be set flush left or centred. The minimum length story for subheads has six paragraphs, since at least two subheads must appear if any are used, and there should be at least two paragraphs below each sub head.

Each subhead is, in effect, a miniature headline for the paragraph it precedes. It should summarise the key thought of that paragraph and it must follow all applicable headline standards.

**Two-deck Headlines:** A headline that contains one complete thought is called a single-deck headline. Each deck may have one, two or three lines but it always has its own 'subject' and 'predicate' and states a complete idea.

Occasionally, two-deck headlines may be desired in these situations:

1.  When the top deck is a banner or spread and the story is only one or two columns wide, a second deck helps the reader's eye locate the story.

2.  Some papers use two-deck headlines on major front-page stories. In this style, both decks are flush left but the second is indented slightly.

A few special rules control the writing of two-deck headlines. First, each deck is complete in itself. Next, the second deck does not repeat the first but introduces a new idea, not quite so important as the thought in the first deck. And finally, no major word is repeated in either deck.

## Reading the Headlines

More than any other words in your entire newspaper, the headlines are the focus and intended to be read widely. The language and the manner adopted in them to flash current news carves an impression on your mind such that you form your opinion on the basis of these reports. They have indelible impact on the psyche of the reader. Therefore, as you look at a newspaper's front page, you not only indulge in reading but your thought process also gets ignited.

- At best, a headline is a greatly abbreviated summary. Its facts are not to be considered representative of the entire story and all its details. Additional facts, which may completely change the headline's impact on you, will be presented as the story is developed.

- In addition to making you jump to the wrong conclusions concerning a news item, a poorly written headline may even cause you to act unwisely. Careless wording may add to the confusion caused by poor selection of information in the preparation of the headline. If the information is of any importance to you, you should read the entire story.

- Technical difficulties in the writing of the headline may interfere with clear understanding of the story. For instance, to save space, a headline writer may use the word 'choose' to mean 'nominate'. Good headline writers try to make each word express the precise meaning they wish to convey, but unit counting and the pressure of deadlines sometimes forces them to do hasty work despite their best intentions.

- Definite slant may creep into the headline. Some daily newspapers feature crime, accidents, sordidness or brutality in major headlines as a publicity gimmick in an effort to sell more papers. When you buy one of these papers, you sometimes have difficulty in finding the relevant headlined incident, because it is given such little eminence in the complete story. But in most papers that do not follow this practice, the headline writer's personal feelings may unconsciously influence his selection and treatment of facts.

- The placement of a story and its headline on a page reflects an editor's or makeup man's judgement. Your own standards of news values may not be the same as his, yet you are influenced by his ideas when you notice the size and placement of various headlines.

□□□

# Planning Interesting Pages

Just as a shopkeeper uses models, artwork and eye-catching arrangements for his products to attract customers to his store, so the newspaperman uses various styles and sizes of fonts, pictures, and other artwork to make every story more readable and interesting to all readers.

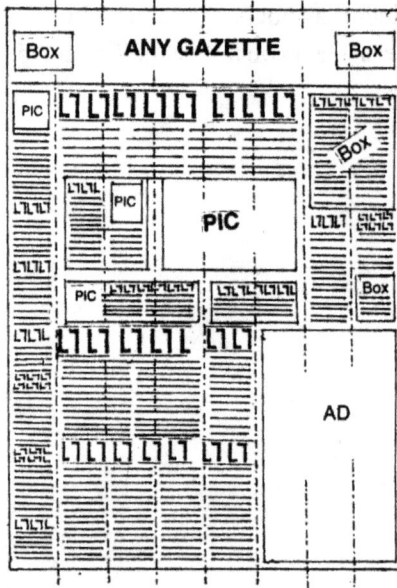

*Specimen Dummy of an 8-Column Newspaper*

If each page of a newspaper were a solid mass of small fonts, with only a cut-off rule between stories, you would find that the newspaper

138

is really dull and uninteresting. Most of the stories would be 'buried' on each page, and you would soon conclude that nothing interesting was happening in the world.

The newspaper makeup man has several important purposes in his plans for the pages of his publication:

- To display every story effectively, according to its importance and interest

- To produce a pleasing effect so that the reader will like the appearance of the paper

- To arrange various elements on each page so that the reader's eyes will be carried from story to story in all the columns from top to bottom

- To make the paper easy to read

In this chapter, you will be the makeup man. Step by step, you will learn the fundamental principles that newspaper people follow as they create attractive and interesting pages in their constant endeavour to enhance their circulation.

### How to Plan Page Makeup

### Step 1 – Balance

The following are layouts for three perfectly balanced front pages. If you draw an imaginary vertical line in the middle of each page, you can see that each mass of font and each headline on the left has its exact counterpart on the right.

While you can get some effective patterns with perfectly balanced pages, the fact remains that news just does not happen in perfect balance. This is because:

1. Stories of perfectly equal size are not at all likely to occur in any given period of time.

2. Even if two stories have equal value, it is not likely that you can get exactly the same amount of information about each.

3. Even if the reporter can get an equal number of facts connected with two stories, it is not likely that he will use exactly the same number of words in writing each.

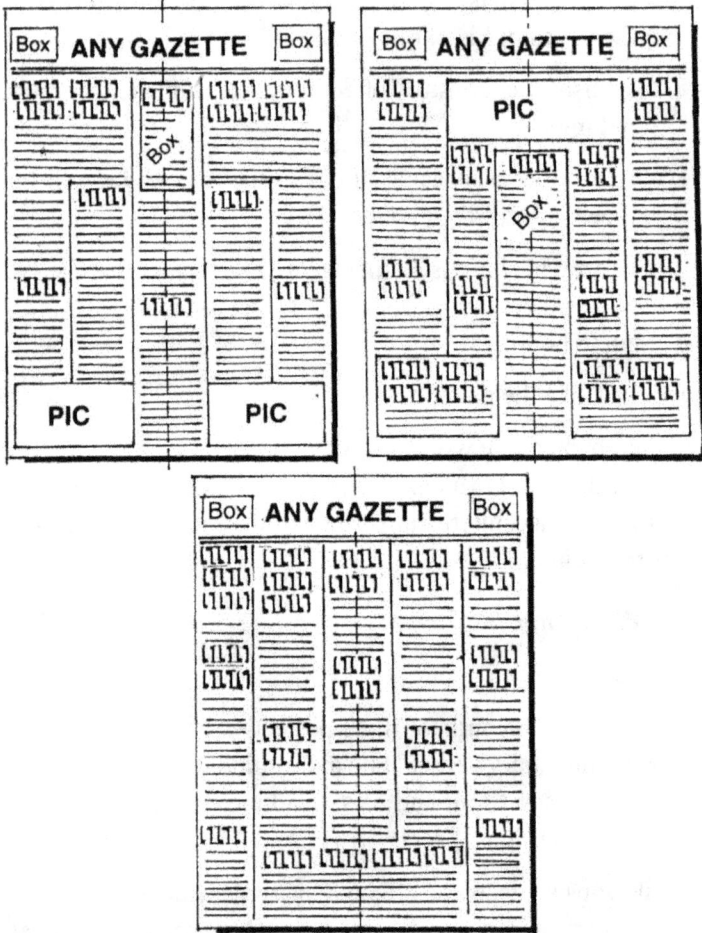

4. If the purpose of the editor is to display stories effectively so that readers are attracted to them, he is making a mistake in laying out perfectly balanced pages. On such pages, the readers see attractive patterns rather than effectively displayed news stories and features.

In building the front page of a newspaper, the editor thinks first in terms of the weight (not kgs, of course) of the masses, of fonts, the headlines, and the pictures with which he is working. For example, President Clinton is arriving in India on Friday night. Here is something that should receive heavy coverage in the paper. Because of its importance, it is worth considerable space. You may say that it can easily overbalance everything else on the page. However, there will be other important stories that will also deserve attention on the front page.

*Germany's Rheinische Post and Ukraine's Kiyevskiy Telegraph offer perfect balance in these instances*

## Step 2 – Informal Balance

Before you try making any pages, here are some helpful suggestions:

- Place the most important stories at the top of the page. Most authorities say that the major story should start in the upper right-hand corner. People usually read the banner headline across the page to the right corner, then down the outside column. Frequently, the story that is second in importance appears at the top left-hand corner of the page.

- After locating the number one story, keep in mind an imaginary vertical line down the centre of the page. If you feel there is too much 'weight' on one side of the page, try to use some element on the other side to provide an informal sort of balance. In the following illustrations, the complete page layouts are not given. Only major elements are shown (Fig. 1).

- While setting a good display for the main stories at the top of the page, see that you do not neglect the bottom and centre of the page. A newspaper is usually folded across the middle. Also remember that in home, the paper would lie bottom side up at least 50 per cent of the time. If the bottom half of the paper is to attract attention, it must have as much 'punch' as the top.

- To give both halves of the page maximum effectiveness, make sure no head is placed at the centre fold. This would separate the story from its headline.

- In using art (photographs and drawings) avoid placing it on the centre fold. Never use one-column pictures there. Use multicolumn pictures only when the fold will not destroy the focal centre of the photo that is the most interesting and absorbing.

- To develop a variety of front layouts, some papers use a 'floating' nameplate (the title name of the newspaper, also called the flag or masthead).

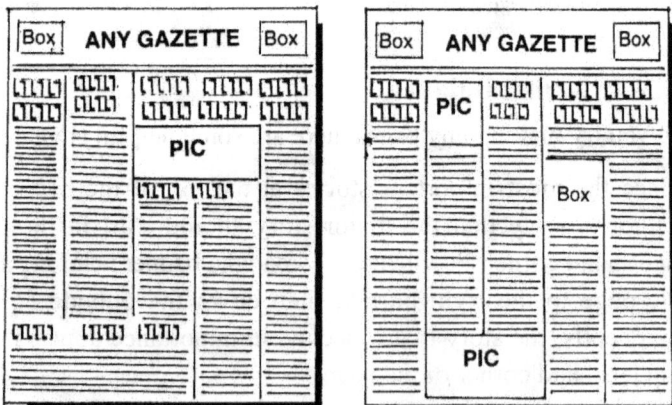

*Fig. 1*

*Page layout of two gazettes*

142

Instead of running the nameplate across the top of the page in a five-column width, they place the nameplate in various positions on the page by changing it to four-column, three-column, and even two-column widths. The value of a floating nameplate is in the variety it offers in makeup. "Nothing is as dead as yesterday's newspaper", therefore, today's must look as different as possible. Remember that, in building the bottom of each page, you must also keep the basic principles of balance in mind.

*Some examples of informal balance*

A special feature can sometimes be run at the top of the page above the nameplate, as shown in the following illustrations (Fig. 2).

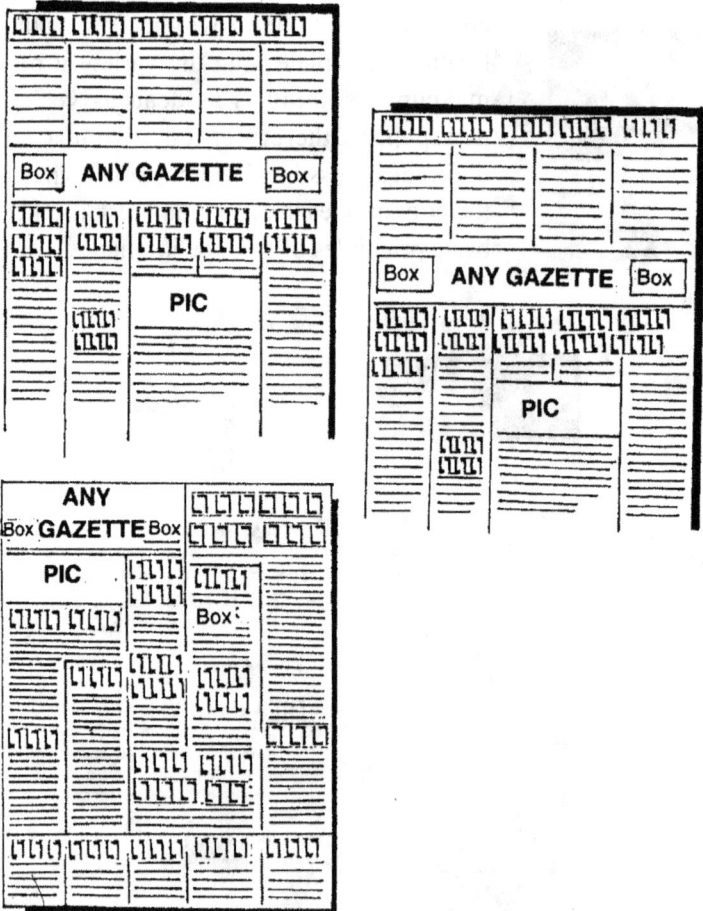

*Fig.2: The special features in these page layouts are taken above the nameplates.*

At the right, the same page is shown with top matter set in four columns to the page instead of five. Below the nameplate, the regular five columns may be used or a feature may be run across the bottom of the page for special effects, as in the illustration.

The makeup man must study his page and calculate the probable reader interest in the same way as does the supermarket manager, who determines where the average housewife will walk in his store as she shops. This is where he will place his bargains. The staples will be off the beaten path because Mrs. Housewife will seek them out anyway. This is a good tip for the newspaperman as he anticipates the eye traffic on his page.

## Movement of the Page

As you build a newspaper page, you must endeavour with the arrangement of the elements to guide the reader's eyes down and across to most of the stories on the page. In other words, the page must have what is called 'movement'. No set rule can be given to guide, but as you look at a page of a paper, note the direction in which your eyes move over the page.

A well-known expert says the optical centre of the page is just above the actual centre, where a quarter-fold meets. By placing your hand here, he says, you will cover the 'danger zone' of your page – the zone, which is hardest to lead the reader to. This always merits special attention by the makeup editor. When a story with a multicolumn head is located on the outside of a page, it is advisable to drop the body type down in the outside column. As you do this, you avoid getting grey matter towards this 'danger zone'.

In considering eye traffic on a page, it is good to remember that an eye has just as much energy to use and when that energy is gone, the reader without realising why lays his paper aside. To conserve eye energy and thereby have more of your page read, avoid 'deadhead' trips for the eye.

Papers, for instance, used to put over lines on photos. They found, however, that when the eye had examined the picture, it went to the over-line then wandered off without reading the caption. A simple device provided the solution to this problem: the over-line was put over the caption, and almost automatically, the eye went down toward the caption.

Do not lead the reader off the page. This is particularly applicable where photos are concerned, have the people in the picture face into the page or make the suggested movement work into the page.

**Horizontal Makeup:** Many modern newspapers avoid the use of a number of long, vertical columns that tend to divide the page into five (or more) long strips. Instead they use many two-column, three-column and even wider features that tend to break up the page into what we might call 'Horizontal' units. Thus, as the eye moves towards the end of a story, it is caught by another horizontal unit and travels back and forth down the page, rather than to the bottom of the page in a single column.

Horizontal makeup is the key to making your newspaper appear easy to read – a point of utmost importance today, with other media competing for the reader's time. Tests show that when a matter is placed before a one-column fashion, he will estimate it will take him ten minutes to read. When the same matter is put under a two-column head, he will estimate eight minutes. When a three-column head is used, he thinks he has only five minutes of reading there. It looks easier. If the makeup man handles this odd measure tool tactfully, he can persuade the reader to read the entire text at the same time saving much of his time.

Caution: Care must be taken not to overdo the horizontal effect and create a helter-skelter sort of 'circus poster' make up. Also, keep in mind that you should seek a fair balance as you move down the pages, avoiding the use of heavy units on one side that are not balanced by units of equivalent weight on the other side.

Look at the given three of the pages illustrated previously. They are marked with lines and arrows to indicate probable eye movement down and across the page.

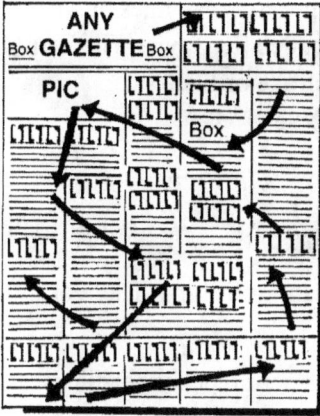

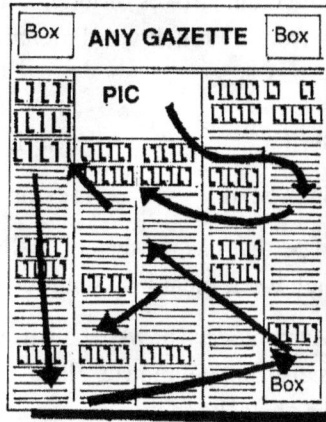

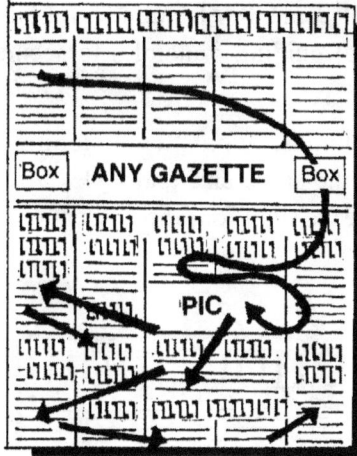

## Step 3 – Make Use of the Principle of Contrast

The next basic principle in developing good layouts for newspapers is contrast. This principle is tied very closely with that of balance.

An understanding of some of the elements of typography is necessary in applying the principle of contrast in newspaper layout.

**Headline Type:** Most newspapers adopt one typeface for use in headlines because it produces a uniform appearing paper. Within this typeface, there are numerous fonts, which can be generally divided into two types: Serif and Sans Serif. If a type has cross-lines or strokes that cross the main strokes of letters, it is called Serif type. The word Serif comes from a French word meaning stroke or line.

$$\mathbf{T} \rightarrow \text{Serif}$$

| | | | | |
|---|---|---|---|---|
| Serif | → | In Serif Font | **T** | **R** |
| Sans Serif | → | In Sans Serif Font | T | R |

Type that has no serifs is called sans-serif type. The word sans is a French word meaning 'without'.

Many modern newspapers use sans-serif type for headlines, as they are precise and geometric, clean and open. They read well and have the flavour of sleek machinery and crisp architecture.

In the use and placement of headlines and body type, the editor should follow several guiding principles to secure proper contrast, variety and balance:

a. In adjoining columns, avoid 'tomb stoning', that means, use of headlines of the same size and style of type. Tomb stoning causes two stories to fight for proper attention, which neither one really receives.

b. In adjoining columns, never place one story alongside another of the same length. It is better to alternate heads and body type.

c. Wherever headlines have to appear together in adjoining columns vary the style of type for contrast.

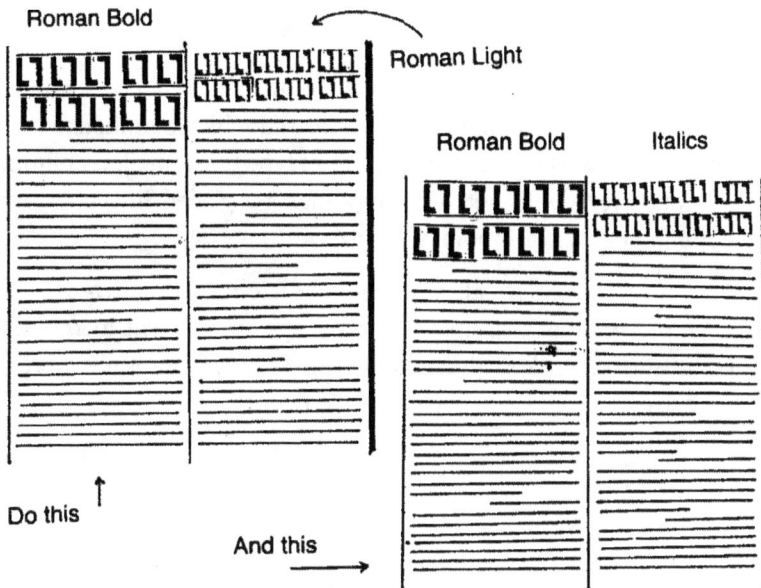

Roman Bold

Roman Light

Roman Bold          Italics

Do this

And this

d. Avoid using double-column (or triple-column) heads in adjoining columns, even if you vary the style and size of headline type.

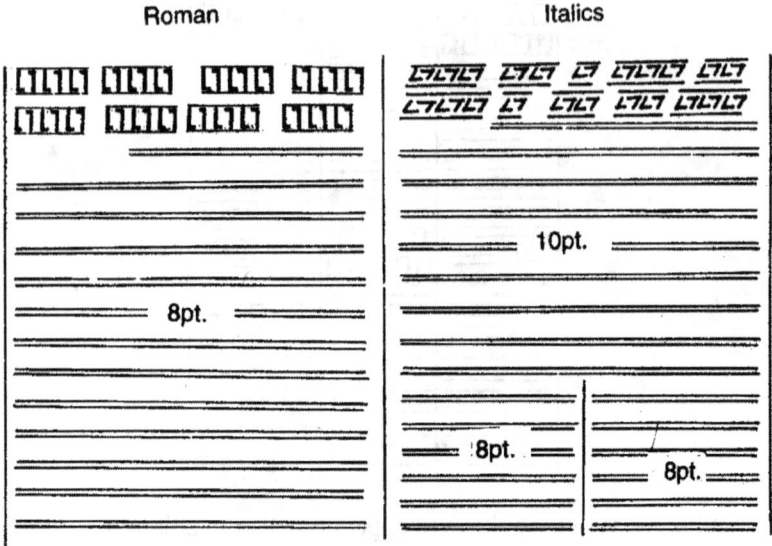

Roman                                    Italics

8pt.                                      10pt.

                                          8pt.        8pt.

e.  If you use a two-column headline, it is usually better to set about six lines of story in 10 points (font size) double column, and then continue the rest of the story in 8 point type down the left column. Another story with headline may then be placed in the second column under the 10 point type size.

f.  Do not set one-column headline immediately under a two-column headline without using some body type in between to provide contrast. Neither headline will get satisfactory attention if there is no body type difference between the two. (Fig. 3)

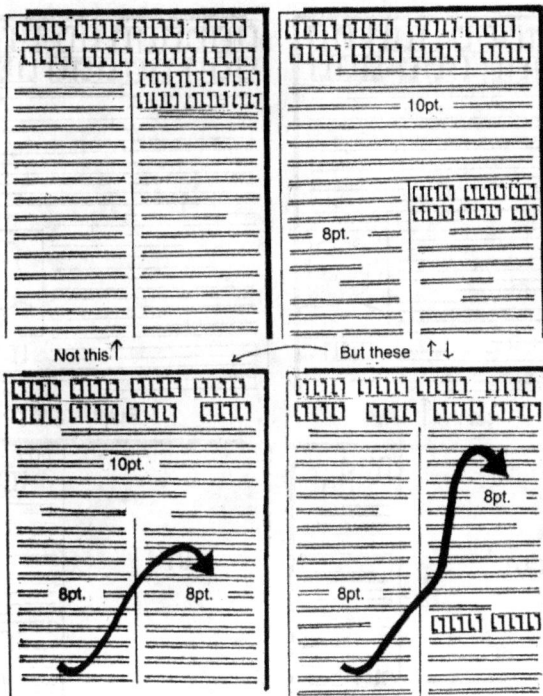

*Fig. 3*

g.  Do not place two unrelated cuts next to each other or a box next to a cut. Separate them at least one column of type.

Since you will probably be limited in the number of cuts available, it is even better to place one cut at the top and the other at the bottom of the page in positions that balance.

h.  If you use a thumbnail (1/2 column) cut, have the face turned toward the copy in the story (if the cut is a side view). Do not place a thumbnail cut next to any other cut. Separate it from another cut by half a column of type. (Fig.4)

151

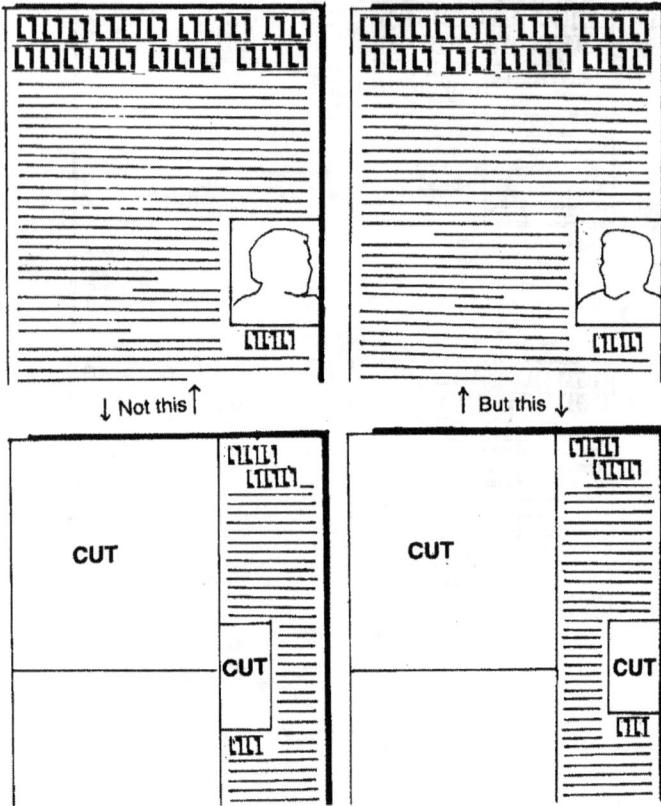

*Fig. 4*

i.  Use few, if any, headlines in all capital letters. Such headlines are more difficult to read than those set in caps and lower case.

| KAPIL VARMA TO HEAD | | Kapil Varma to head the |
| THE COMMISSION | | Commission |

### Step 4 – Make use of the Principle of Variety

The next basic principle in developing good layouts is variety. An understanding of what makes good balance and contrast will help provide variety in makeup. However, some additional points should be made.

While the basic headlines for most stories consist of two and three lines, a variety of headlines (if not overdone) will provide interesting looking stories and pages. You should study city newspapers for headline examples. Some city tabloid newspapers (which are usually of five-column width) make considerable use of unusual types of heads.

Observe the illustrations of interesting and unusual heads that follow.

a.

Kicker

Banner Headline

Kicker

3 Col. Headline

b.

3/4" Box Above Head

c.

2 Col., 24-PT. Head

14-PT. Pyramid
Second Deck
Asterisks

153

d. **2 Lines 18-Pt. Roman** — **2 or 3 Words 24-Pt. Italics or Script**

e. — Kickers Above and Below Main Headline

f. — Short Question Leading Into Main Headline

g. **3 Col., 30-Pt. Head Story Starts Here**

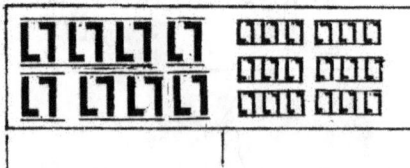

2 or 3 Short Words — 2 Col. Box Long Statement in 3 Lines

i. **30-Pt. Head**

**14-pt. Second Deck**

CUT

j.

Head Centered Over 2 Cols. ·with Typographic Device and Top Box

k. **2 or 3 Words**

**2 Col. Rules**

l.

Short Heads Centered over Double-Col. Text, with Box Rules

Variety in page makeup should be planned from issue to issue. If there is a page editor for each page (many newspapers do have page editors), he can plan a different page layout regularly.

Thorough and consistent coverage by reporters should bring a wide variety of news stories and features to light that will call for new types of display in succeeding issues.

Be careful that in your effort to provide variety in makeup, you do not develop fancy pattern rather than displays that entice the reader's interest. Remember that a fancy pattern calls attention to itself and not to the stories on the page.

### Step 5 – Plan Attractive Inside Pages

Although the front page of your newspaper is the showcase for the stories of widest interest, you must do your best to make the inside pages attractive. Most publications follow two principal arrangements of advertisements that offer best opportunity for display of your ads and also for display of your news and feature stories.

155

**Half-Pyramid Arrangement of Advertising:** One theory behind the half-pyramid arrangement is that a person reads down the page through the news, and then his eyes wander on the advertisement copy that touches the story. The largest advertisements are in the lower right-hand corner because they will probably be seen even though they are partially surrounded by other, smaller ads.

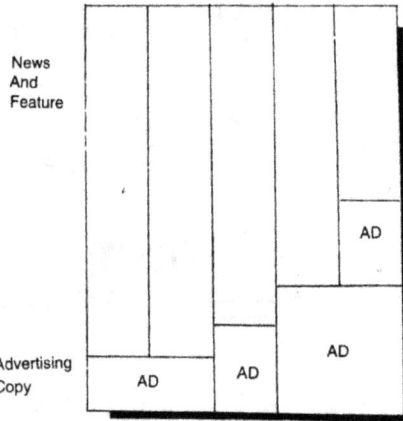

Notice the 'half-pyramid' arrangement of advertisements on this page of *The Times of India.*

With the half-pyramid arrangement of ads, the top-left space provides the best display for the most important or unusual story on the page. Consequently, plans for the display of news material generally start in the upper left corner.

a.  Start with a picture tied to the big story. Perhaps ads are to appear in the lower-right corner of the page. This, of course, would make a well-balanced complete page impossible. Therefore, after spotting the main story, you will have to make good use of contrast and variety rather than balance. Note the given illustrations of interesting page layouts.

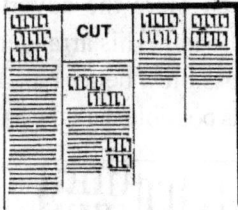

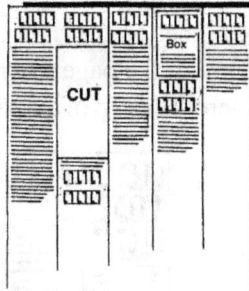

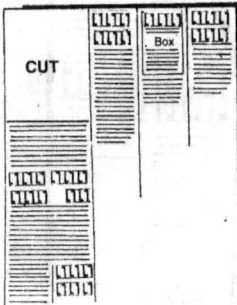

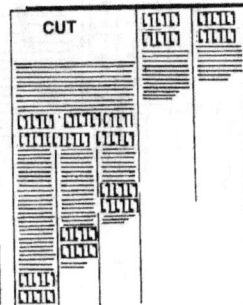

b. If there are no pictures available, you can use other devices to gain contrast and variety. For example, use a kicker above a two or three-column head. Use a box. Use boxed heads.

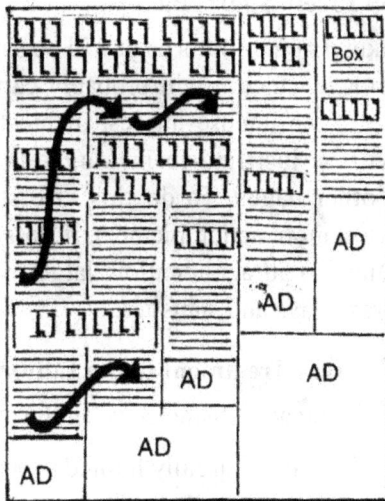

**'Well' Arranged Advertisements:** Here the advertising copy should be higher on the right than on the left. This arrangement opens up the centre of the page and makes possible a better balance of news elements across the top of the page than is possible with the half-pyramid.

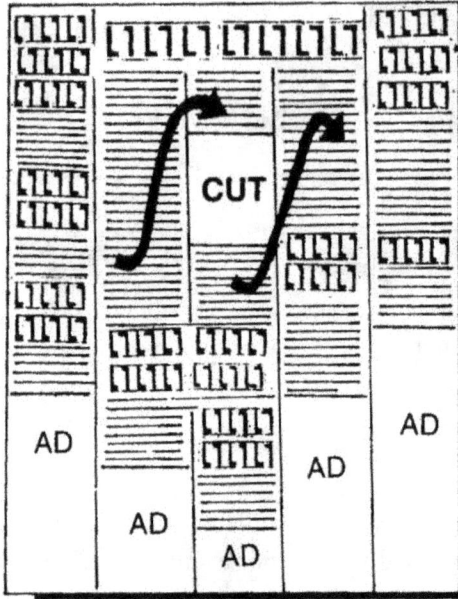

## Step 6 – Develop Lively Sports Page

In general, the makeup of the sports page will be similar to that of any other inside news page, since it will probably carry advertisements. However, because of the intense interest of most readers in sports activities, you will be justified in making this page 'noisier' in appearance than other pages. To do this, use streamer heads for outstanding victories, more action pictures, if possible, more unusual typographical devices to attract attention, larger types for headlines, tabulations of scores, plays and statistics.

## Step 7 – Give Different Treatment to the Editorial Page

If possible, avoid putting advertising copy on the editorial page.

Since copy on this page is usually limited to editorials and special features, more literary in nature than regular news stories, the page should be given a typographical treatment different from that given to other pages.

It has been customary to place the editorial page in an inside position in the newspaper, usually page 2. However, more and more editorial pages are being given preferred positions in newspapers across the country. Many have been moved to the back page. One daily newspaper that made this move found that letters to the editor increased by 50 per cent, a definite proof of higher reader interest.

Here are several points that should be noted in planning editorial pages:

- Headlines should be less bold than on other pages. Use more lightface and italic types.

- By careful planning, you can vary the width of columns on the page. Instead of having the type set in five columns, you might make all columns wider and have only four columns. Or you can set some columns wider than others if you plan very carefully. However, remember that if you depart from your regular column width, you create problems in page makeup. You cannot use material from other pages as last-minute filler nor can you transfer material easily from one space to another on the page.

The customary position for editorials is the upper left hand space. You can vary from custom but you should consistently use the same place for editorials so that readers will know where to look for the newspaper's editorial opinions. Editorials are often set in larger type than regular body type so that they can be read more easily. Lines should be given plenty of breathing space, with extra lead between lines. More than the usual space may separate paragraphs. All these devices give your editorials a special character of their own, so that they are easily recognised.

The masthead, containing the title of the publication, the names of staff members and other information probably should be placed at the bottom of the page in an inconspicuous position. Newspapers placed the masthead at the left above the editorials as a matter of practice.

However, since the masthead is included as a matter of necessity and not because it has special interest for the reader, it should not be placed in a position of greater reader interest.

Line drawings, such as editorial cartoons, tie in well with the lighter appearance of the editorial page. Dark photographs may well be reserved for other pages, although you should not necessarily eliminate photos if they would be appropriate. The two-line drawings shown below illustrate interesting use of varying column widths, cuts, features, columns, and other material appropriate to an editorial page.

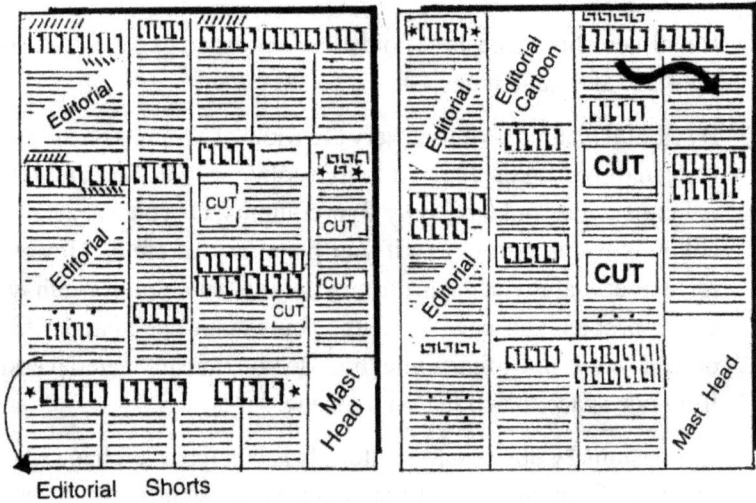

Editorial    Shorts

□□□

# Pictures for the Paper

Almost every printed publication adds to the effectiveness of its material with illustrations. Catalogues of large mail-order houses have photographs and drawing of the products. Magazines use pictures freely and some pictorial magazines tell their stories almost entirely with photographs. Large number of business firms no longer present their annual reports in the form of cold statistics. Pictures of activities and successful achievements within the plant or district, as well as of social activities among the employees help present facts about the business more effectively.

## The Chief Editor of Photo Section Must Plan and Schedule All Pictures

Someone from your newspaper must regulate the schedule of getting pictures, which are appropriate, interesting and of the highest quality. Many newspapers have picture editors to direct the planning, arranging, developing and taking of all pictures with the assistance, of course, of photographers.

The editor of photo section must confer with all page editors in determining what photographs or pictures should be used on each page. For every page, they will discuss the stories that are to be run and decide which stories best lend themselves to illustrations. The picture editor must be ready with numerous suggestions regarding the type of pictures likely to be most interesting. He should plan for two or three feature-type pictures that might be used on any page as stories in themselves because sometimes scheduled pictures turn out poorly in spite of all the care taken by the photo section editor and the photographer.

The picture editor must schedule all pictures. Above all, the picture editor must be a persistent type of person who constantly checks the day-to-day progress and follows through to make absolutely certain that there is no slip. When deadline arrives, there must be no failures. The pictures must be ready.

When planning his schedule, the picture editor must bear in mind that he has to be ahead of the news staff. He must work several days ahead of them. His schedule should constantly operate almost a week ahead of that of the news writing staff.

## Taking and Making Pictures

Anyone can take a picture. It's easy. Just find a subject, aim the camera and trip the shutter. Your processing house will take care of the rest. Of course, the finished product may disappoint you. But whether you have cut off the subject's head, failed to allow for extra bright sunlight or neglected to focus correctly, you are nevertheless, a picture-taker.

A good photographer is also a picture-maker but a somewhat different person. He has learned how to handle his camera skilfully. He understands that good pictures are the result of careful attention to detail. Furthermore, he knows that timing and composition are the most essential elements of photography, and he works hard to inject imagination into the pictures he takes. In short, the photographer is an artist.

Important points one should take care of:

- Choose the right equipment.
- Get a clear and sharp image.
- Decide what you want in your picture.
- Tell a story with every picture.
- Capture the spirit of the occasion.
- Crop unnecessary areas.
- Write an interesting and complete caption.
- File all pictures after publication.

□□□

# Advertising

A person needs certain qualities to be a successful advertising salesman. Actually, most of these qualities make for success in any line of work. The salesman must be:

1.  **Dependable:** The advertising salesman must be able to stick to the business when sent to call on prospects. If he has an appointment with a prospective advertiser, he must reach there on time. He should live up to promises and follow through on all details because he has a sense of responsibility towards both the advertiser and the paper.

2.  **Honest:** A good salesman makes only accurate representations concerning his paper. He never makes careless promises or misleading statements.

3.  **Persistent:** The salesman makes use of every reasonable sales point that he can. If the prospective advertiser is not convinced and denies him business after the salesman has done his best, he tries to analyse the cause of his failure, thinks up new sales points, designs a better sample ad to present and tries again for the next issue.

4.  **Courteous:** The salesman remembers that he is representing his newspaper and reacts courteously regardless of what the person may say. He always thanks the person if he makes a sale and does not forget to thank him for his interest if a sale is not made.

5.  **Resourceful:** The salesman must know his sales points so well that he is able to answer objections by pointing out new ways in which

the prospective advertiser will benefit by advertising in the paper. If he thinks he cannot sell the prospect, he asks another salesman to try with a different approach, if possible. He may design a new ad copy to submit if the prospective advertiser does not care for his first sample.

6. **Observant:** Even as he walks through the store or the office to see the prospective advertiser, the salesman should note details about the display of products or gather information of the services that he may be able to use in his sales talk. He may spot some item that he feels will prompt the readers to 'go for' if it is advertised in the paper. He may get some idea of what the prospective advertiser is trying to 'push' at the time and may suggest that the item be advertised. As he talks to him, he makes a mental note of information that may be valuable to the other salesmen in the future.

7. **Eager to work and learn:** An advertising space seller (as a newspaper ad man is also known as) must have potentiality to learn the right mechanisms to sell space to the prospective advertisers, as they provide the revenue to the newspaper agency. Advertising is the backbone of a publication as it generates revenue to carry business smoothly.

8. **Friendly:** A space seller should like talking to people and must be interested in developing cordial and long-term relations. He must be willing to let the other person talk and must be sympathetic to his problems. He must be eager to help the other person, if possible. He must remember that advertising in his newspaper may help the prospective advertiser increase his business. And most important of all, he must be proud of his paper and must entertain an ardent desire to establish best of relations between the advertiser and the people connected with his paper.

## Planning an Advertising Campaign

No newspaper can be financially successful unless it has a well-organised staff and a meticulously planned method of procedure. There is nothing accidental or haphazard in the sales approach of the advertising staff. Before a salesman calls on a prospect, he has had a thorough training in three vital areas. First, he becomes thoroughly familiar with the background of his newspaper and can offer important information concerning its finances, its circulation, its space requirements and its advertising rates. Second, he searches out vital size of his business and his potential advertising needs. Finally, he learns the best and most effective way of presenting himself, his newspaper and his proposed advertising plans.

You can master these important skills if you follow a logical sequence of procedures.

## Step A – Organise Your Advertising Prospects and Salesmen's Beats

The territory covered by the newspaper should be organised and demarcated so that each salesman has his own area to cover and there is no duplication of effort. This also saves time.

Consider the following two basic plans for organisation of territory.

1.  The advertising manager may divide the business district by streets or by sections of town, assigning a specific area to each salesman. If this plan is followed, the advertising manager must know in advance where the major prospects are located and try to assign an equal number of good prospects to each member of his staff.

2.  The advertising manager may group all the local business firms according to type, listing these on assignment sheets accordingly. With this method each salesman may specialise in one type of business or perhaps handle multiple domains.

Whichever method of organisation you decide on, prepare your plan in permanent form, so that it serves as a guide, not only for the present staff but also for future staff. You will save them considerable time in getting organised if you keep this record.

In determining beats, whether by territory or by groups of firms, remember that it may be advisable for salesmen to occasionally shift prospects. One salesman may be unsuccessful with some firms for one reason or another. He may then suggest to the advertising manager

165

that he might do better with other firms originally assigned to another salesman. Or he may feel that another salesman might be able to make a sale where he was not able to do so.

It is important that each salesman always covers his beat thoroughly and turns in detailed work reports for every day on the job.

## Step B – Prepare a Prospect Card

After you complete your preliminary survey of the territory and the prospect list, your next step should be to design a handy prospect card, to be filled out continuously as you work throughout the year. This card should contain any information you feel may be of assistance, especially to future advertising salesman. The sample card shown here suggests the type of information you should be gathering and recording.

### PROSPECT CARD

STORE                       ADDRESS

_____

BEST TIME TO SEE

_____

USUAL SIZE OF AD      FREQUENCY OF AD

_____

TIMES OF YEAR THE STORE ADVERTISES MOST

_____

BRANDS OF GOOD USUALLY HANDED BY THE STORE

_____

## Step C – Determine Your Selling Points

Now that you have your list of prospects and have filled in suitable blanks for building a permanent prospect file, you are ready to go to work. Not yet. What are you going to say when you meet the prospective advertiser, whether he is in the office or at sales counter?

First, you must be convinced that you represent a newspaper of high quality if you are to convince your prospect that this is true. To do this, you should be familiar with the paper's record. Second, you must also know basic selling points and be convinced of their truth.

## Step D – Determine Your Advertising Rates

You must know your paper's advertising rates. If your paper already has an established policy on rates, you must work out a basic advertising rate. This can be done in either of the following ways:

- Charge a flat rate per column centimetre for all advertising, regardless of size or number of insertions. When this plan is successful, the paper can get a maximum income from the use of a minimum of space. If the charge per column cm is reasonable, advertisers usually have little objections to the rates.

- Have a sliding scale of charges. A 4-centimetre ad inserted in one issue costs a certain amount – for example Rs. 50. If the advertiser agrees to carry this ad for a number of issues, the price per insertion is lowered. Or, if the advertiser carries a larger ad, the rate is less per column centimetre. If he carries a larger ad for several issues, the price per column centimetre may be still lower.

## Step E – A Salesman should be Familiar with Advertising Terms

When the salesman starts out, he should be familiar with terminology commonly used by printers and advertising people. Some of the terms are in general newspaper use and have appeared elsewhere in this text. However, you find it useful to have two terms that are applicable to advertising grouped here for quick reference so that you may apply them to your advertising needs.

- A cut is any illustration used in an ad. In newspapers printed by the letterpress method, all illustrations are printed from metal or plastic plates prepared by an engraver from photographs or drawings.

- A tear sheet is a single page torn from the paper and presented to the advertiser as a proof that his ad has been run correctly.

## Step F – Prepare to Go into the Field

Before going in the field be prepared with the following:

- Advance sales letter (send it beforehand)
- Previous issues of newspapers, copies of your sales contract, copies of your rate card etc
- Neat and pleasing appearance
- And above all, courtesy and politeness

## Special Ad Ideas

While the regular advertising is the backbone of your paper, valuable revenue is gained through unique ideas that are gained out of special features in the neighbourhood. A resourceful advertising staff can discover many special events or ideas on which to build 'promotions' and add to the paper's income. These promotions often add interest to an otherwise 'ordinary' issue.

## Tie-in Ads

Entire groups of ads may be tied in around special events or features, such as the opening of the cricket season, the big play, an important tourist festival and so on.

## A Shopping Column

A regular shopping column, with brief listings of 'specials' or outstanding items can be a popular feature of your paper, as well as a good source of revenue. Special advertising rates will have to be established for this type of material and the person writing the column must prepare his matter carefully and well in advance.

□□□

# Frequently Asked Questions

## A. Electronic Journalism

### 1. How is the job market in Electronic Journalism?

**Answer:** We frequently turn to television, radio and their websites for news and information. Whether the economy is good or bad, news, which is a vital element of our daily lives, will always be in demand.

And just like journalists of the print media, journalists from the electronic media also fill this demand. From reporters, photographers and producers to managers and anchors, their job is to transmit the 'actuality' of the sights and sounds of events as they happen.

In 2003, an estimated 80,000 people were working in different news and news related programmes at commercial TV and radio stations in the nation. This number is estimated to grow further to at least 1,50,000 in the coming years. Hence definitely there is no dearth of jobs in the Electronic Media.

### 2. Where do the 'Electronic Journalists' work?

**Answer:** 'Electronic Journalists' typically work at the following places:

- **Commercial TV stations** provide the maximum number of jobs. News staffers typically range from 10-20 people in small regional and local channels while national channels have a staff of at least 250-300. A few employ still more.

- Commercial radio stations early in the 21st century were sadly losing newsrooms and jobs to industry consolidation and technology. However, in the last years, the coming up of new FM channels have boosted the audience confidence on the radio and in turn strengthened the field. In our country, most of the villagers still prefer radio, because of its portability and cost. Hence, job opportunities in both the commercial radio stations and public radio stations are immense and increasing rapidly.

- Public television, which in our nation is known as 'Doordarshan', offers alternatives to regular commercial fare. Doordarshan also offers solid content in its programmes and has more than 30 regional channels under its aegis which it manages itself, including the now famous Doordarshan offshoots – DD Sports and DD News.

- Public radio stations under the AIR (All India Radio) definitely are the largest employers of radio journalists in the nation.

- Networks, various 24-hour news broadcast multilingual channels, employ several thousand news people.

- Local cable systems in a number of larger cities, maintain news operations with staff to cover 'hyper-local' news, which essentially takes place within the communities covered by the local cable station.

- The Web includes sites maintained by most TV and many radio stations. Keeping a site up-to-date is usually the job of a news producer.

The following are related fields where an electronic journalist might find work:

- Wire services such as the Press Trust of India, Associated Press and Reuters employ hundreds of journalists to provide news to broadcast stations and newspapers.

- News feed services provides stations with specialised audio and video on news, sports, weather, business, traffic and other audience interest areas.

- Syndication services sell stations news programme inserts on such topics as health, law, personal finances, consumer awareness, sports and entertainment. Like news feed services, they need specialised journalists.

- Corporate television is a growing field utilising specialists trained in news. Its varied projects include the production of videos and programmes for such uses as sales and staff training. Large businesses send programmes they produce to workers on the job within the same buildings or by communication satellite to locations anywhere in the world.

- Public relations help industries, organisations and government tell their stories to the public. PR often seeks employees who are experienced in broadcast news.

### 3. What are the various opportunities in Electronic Journalism?

**Answer:** An electronic journalist's first job will probably be more than one. He/she may report, shoot video, produce the TV package and do a Web version all on the same story. Multiple duty assignments, common in small stations, are today a trend in stations of all sizes. Versatility and flexibility are indeed keys to getting a job and developing journalistic talents. The more things you can do, the better.

Keeping in mind that the same person may serve as two or more of the following, here are some of the people or positions:

**Anchor (also known as newscaster):** An anchor is an on-air coordinator of a news programme. Also a host and reporter, the anchor reads news stories, introduces reports by others and may interview news sources live. An anchor weaves the programme together for listeners and viewers. News, sports and weather anchors meanwhile interact with him/her as a team. An anchor may also serve as a programme's managing editor or producer, and may report from the scene of news events.

**Reporter:** A reporter covers news stories, usually on camera or tape and from the scene or the newsroom. Reporters develop sources and interview newsmakers. They also gather information from wire services, periodicals and computerised databases. Once information has been gathered, they narrate the story in words, sound and video inputs. They often report live from the news scene without any pre-prepared script or even notes. Many reporters also do some anchoring. This goes on to prove that most anchors come up from the ranks of reporters.

**Photographer (photojournalist, cameraperson):** These professionals are operators of electronic cameras used in video reporting of news. They may also do some reporting, especially in smaller operations. A photographer/cameraperson also edits or helps edit tape or digital video-audio at many stations. As cameras become more compact and easier to use, stations are increasingly using 'one-person bands' which means that the same person shoots and reports the story, combining journalistic and photographic skills.

**Assignment Editor:** The Assignment Editor is essentially a coordinator who keeps a track of scheduled and unscheduled news events and assigns beats and duties to reporters and photographers to cover them. He/she also monitors police radio broadcasts and takes phone calls from news sources. An assignment editor often has to make quick decisions under time pressure. In some smaller stations, an assignment editor is also supposed to maintain field contact with reporters and photojournalists through two-way radio and/or phone. He/she is the focal point in scheduling and overseeing satellite feeds of news stories. Definitely this job is tough and may be a steppingstone to newsroom management. It is most often a television position, though some large radio stations also have assignment editors.

**News Producer:** A News Producer is a 'behind-the-scenes' journalist who brings together live and taped actualities of events, along with graphics and background information, into a news story, and coordinates stories into news programmes. He/she often writes news stories and lead-ins to them. He/she may also edit tapes, prepare graphics and adapt stories to the station's web site. News producers are definitely creators, decision-makers and often managers who must be expert in many aspects of TV news. They are also prime prospects for higher management positions.

**Executive Producer:** The Executive Producer is an overall supervisor of news producers and coordinator of production elements of news programmes. Often a chief producer of principal news programme, an executive producer works with news director on matters of programme format and content, production financial budget and personnel performance. Executive news producers often move up to become news directors.

**Writer:** Writers essentially are journalists who writes news copy from information gathered from news teletype services, network feeds, field reports, interviews, recordings, and other sources. In typical TV or radio operations, most writing is done by producers, reporters and anchors rather than by separate writers as such.

**Tape Editor:** A Tape Editor is the one who selects and assembles the portions of audio or video tape or digital recording that best tell a news story. Editing is also done by photographers, producers and reporters.

**Multimedia Producer:** Multimedia Producers are in charge of the station's website, keeping it up to date on local news, weather and sports, plus depth coverage perhaps not included in the limited time allotted to the news programmes. Some stations do little of this. Others meanwhile do a lot.

**News Director:** The News Director is a person in charge of a TV or radio news operation. This person who is essentially a 'journalist-manager' sets policies and makes decisions on news coverage and presentation. He also recruits and trains personnel, manages newsroom finances and works with managers of other departments at the station. News directors in radio and small television stations often also do reporting, producing or anchoring.

**Sportscasters and weathercasters:** Sportscasters and weathercasters are part of the news operation at most TV stations and many radio stations. Most stations though usually hire specialists. TV weathercasters are meteorologists more often than journalists, and sportscasters must be expert in sports.

Other news job titles include chief photographer, graphics specialist, assignment desk assistants, assistant and associate producers, special projects producer, newscast director and managing news editor. The position of managing news editor is found mainly in large operations and may range from a programme's chief editor to a news director's second-in-command for news matters.

### 4. What are the salaries and emoluments like in this field?

Well, to be truthful, salaries range from excellent to poor. For the rank and file, salaries lag other fields that normally require a college degree. Annual salaries for anchors and news directors at network affiliated TV stations in the 25 largest cities of nation typically go six digits monthly. But in some small TV stations and in the majority of radio stations, most broadcast news people earn less than their counterparts at newspapers and in other professional positions.

This is normally because an oversupply of job-seeking beginners helps hold salaries down. Expect low pay for a year or two as you gain experience and develop your talents. Then, you should be ready for a substantial salary increase at your station or, more likely, in a move to a larger station.

News directors on an average receive higher salaries than rank and file anchors at most TV stations in small and medium cities.

Producers generally average a little more than reporters in small and medium stations. But the ceiling is higher for those reporters who move up to major stations.

Salaries for most news staff normally run two to three times as high in major TV and radio stations as in small ones.

Generally advancement in salary as one moves up the career ladder is greatest for anchors, reporters and news directors. Least gain comes for producers, assignment editors and other rank and file who work behind the scenes in the newsroom. This is based on my personal experience and may not be a rule in most cases though.

## 5. What are the pros and cons of Electronic Journalism?

All television and radio journalists like their work at least this is what they claim. However, according to a survey carried in 1990s by Radio-Television News Directors Association (RTNDA) in the United States, three-fourths of the nearly 2,200 media professionals who took part in the survey stated they were at least moderately satisfied with their jobs. The remaining were only moderately dissatisfied. Job satisfaction levels were about the same for television and radio.

But the survey also revealed that the majority of the people working in broadcast news had considered quitting the field at some point of time. When asked 'why' they stated the following reasons: stress (from deadlines and other pressures), disturbed family life (the hours can be terrible) and disenchantment with the field (news operations vary widely in quality).

However, when asked what made them like their work, the answer was – It's often exciting. You're in the middle of what's happening. What you do in your job can make a difference in the world around you. It's satisfying to know you're perhaps communicating something important to thousands of people and that you've done a good job of it! If you're on the air, your face and voice will become familiar to your viewers, which may hold appeal for you. Talented and enterprising colleagues also make the job more attractive. Finally, if you move up to a big-time position either on the air or in management, your salary will be very attractive, most probably in six figures.

But then again many radio and television journalists are underpaid. There's a widening gap between the salaries of anchors and news directors and those of the majority of staff. In small and middle markets, the basic news handlers i.e., reporters, photographers and producers have lost ground to the cost of living in recent years. This is due in part to an immense deluge of job applicants. Stations exploit these eager newcomers who are willing to work at minimal salaries to start their careers.

As in other different career options, job security is lesser compared to the old days of local ownership, when stations were not supposed to act as profit machines for corporate owners accountable to stockholders. In recent years, budgetary layoffs and the elimination of whole news departments in extreme cases have become more common.

TV and radio journalists often reported job-related health problems. Stress and fatigue can result from the damaging pressure of taskmasters who are under corporate orders to extract more output with the same or less staff. Again, profits reign supreme, over and above the well being of people whose hard work generates these profits.

Irregular and odd working hours are a norm with broadcast news and often result in marital discord and other personal problems. Frequent travel to various cities on professional assignments and progress are disruptive to family life. Divorces are also quite common.

## 6. Is Electronic Journalism the right career for me?

You must consider all aspects apart from the pros and cons that have been noted above. Seek out professionals already in the field and talk to them. They will welcome your interest in what they do. Assess your natural inclinations and your potential.

Remember you must also be aware of your interests and expectations and analyse what is important to you in a career. It may help to compare your career values to those of journalists now working in the field. Are these your basic expectations from your job in a nutshell:

- Use of your abilities
- Opportunity for originality or initiative
- Challenges
- Excitement
- Opportunity to advance
- Job security
- Job's value input to society

Salary is also a very important consideration.

## 7. Am I suited for a career in Electronic Journalism?

To get ahead in radio or television news, you should be educated, 'journalism' literate, inquisitive, have clear-thinking ability and cool-headedness. You must also be able to get along with people, gather news, interview news sources, write well and (if on-air) tell stories effectively to the listener or viewer. You must develop a sense and nose for news. And to put the news into perspective, you'll need to be well versed in current events and history!

What do bosses look for? What will help you most to get that first job and move ahead:

- General presentation (appearance, business manners, personality, etc.), that counts in any field

- Writing skills and basic communications with words

- Earlier study, training or work experience in broadcasting or cable, internships are a plus

- The duration or extent of hands-on experience in actual work situations; again, the internship or other actual experience counts

- Hands-on experience with technologies (cameras, editing equipment, computers etc.)

What helps most?

When a number of news directors were asked of the stream or line of study in college that had helped them most, they replied:

- Writing

- Other journalism or communication courses

- Social studies (history, government, sociology, etc.)

Unless you work strictly behind the scenes, your voice and appearance must be acceptable for interviews and on-the-spot reports. While golden voices and glamorous faces are not required, you need to communicate clearly, credibly and pleasingly. Broadcast reporters not only cover the news, but also must be able to tell it effectively into a microphone and, for television on a camera.

If you decide upon TV or radio journalism, give it your best and see how it goes. If it does not turn out in your favour, there are many other career options. And your time will have been well invested in any case because it would turn out to be the most fruitful and lifetime experiences for you. Communication skills you develop in radio or TV news will make you more effective in most other occupations.

## 8. How should I prepare for a career in Electronic Journalism?

Develop abilities and skills you will need in your career while you are in high school or college. Learn grammar, composition and clear expression. Mastery of language is a requisite skill set and the foundation of various other aspects of personality development. Experience in public speaking, debate or dramatic arts will help prepare you for on-air reporting. Live reports require you to think and talk instantly and exhibit quick reflexes while on your feet.

Learn to use a computer effectively for typing, information retrieval from the Internet and web construction. Become adept with all digital things.

Read and observe as much as you can about all kinds of people and activities. Don't limit yourself to assigned readings. Read books, magazines and newspapers. Become a knowledgeable listener and viewer of broadcast news.

As soon as you can, start getting experience. Working on a school newspaper can be valuable though only very few schools in India have their own newspapers. Nowadays, large and established names like *The Times of India* and *Hindustan Times* give ample opportunities to students to exhibit their flair with the pen and grow. Participate in debate and performing arts. There may be part-time or freelance work in news, announcing or production at a local radio or TV station. Explore and use your initiative to check the possibilities.

Look into visiting stations in your area and observe their news operations. Call in advance for a convenient time. Tag along with a reporter if possible. See how tape is edited and how news teams put newscasts together. Conduct a self-introspection if you would like this kind of work. Check on opportunities for beginners to gain experience at the stations. Seek guidance from people currently working in news departments about their training procedures and further education on this field.

## College Education

Put broad liberal arts education first in your college or university programme of study. About three-fourths of your courses should be in general studies or arts and sciences that means history, political science, sociology, psychology, economics, literature, fine arts, etc. It's easier to teach skills on the job to an educated person than to educate a skilled practitioner who missed out on liberal arts back in college.

## Picking a College or University

Look for a college or university that is strong in liberal arts and general education, and where students do advanced lab work in actual broadcast or cable news settings rather than being limited to workbooks and 'make believe' labs. News directors favour colleges where students get hands-on training.

Check if your course disperses professional instructions by faculty who have worked in radio or television news. You deserve to be taught by experts. Look also for teachers who keep in contact with the real world of today's radio and TV news operations. Since it is a very fast changing and highly volatile line so much so that a few years away can put a professor out of date.

Look for your money's worth. The price of college education keeps going up. So give prospective colleges a hard look. Some of the best TV/radio journalism programmes are at relatively low cost colleges. Indeed, not all are expensive. Highly reputed colleges/ institutions may be right for your individual needs. A public college or an institution in your own state could be your best choice. At the same time, private colleges and institutions often offer more attractive financial aid packages, which can be really helpful to facilitate higher education.

**Internships**

Internships stand in good stead and pay off during the time of job-hunting. Most employers do not pay a salary during the internships. But they add a credential that helps get you hired. Studies have found that the great majority of applicants who get entry-level jobs have held internships, often at the same station.

It is valuable because you will be able to work in a real news operation, not just a college classroom or lab. Even the best journalism courses usually can do no more than give you a background for the duties involved in getting news on the air, cable or the web. Working as a part of news staff that is competing with others for viewership takes you an important step ahead beyond the campus.

You will also develop a network of professional contacts to help you get a job and later progress in your career. Those contacts count.

## 9. How does one get a job as an electronic journalist?

Most entry-level TV news staff is hired as reporters, photographers or production assistants. Reporting and photojournalism go hand in hand and may be done by the same person. Just shooting video tends to be a low paid, often dead-end job. But the entry-level journalist who can shoot and report the same event, or one who has strong post-production editing skills is a premium candidate and gets preference. Such staff members are cost-efficient from the managerial point of view.

In radio, the initial or first jobs in small and medium markets typically combine reporting and news casting, as may also be the case in large organisations. Working with tape recordings of news events and interviews is required. The radio newscaster normally edits actualities (the sound of newsmakers), writes, edits and produces his or her programme.

Few of the large news operations in major markets such as Mumbai or Chennai hire newcomers who are just out of college. The assignments normally are writing, desk or production assistance, or other inside jobs.

Few start as TV anchors. The first step is usually to prove yourself as a reporter. If you come across well on the air, you may get to do some daytime or weekend anchoring. As you develop, your primary job may become anchoring instead of reporting. And that third step will probably mean a good boost in pay. But you must work up the ladder to it. If you want to go on the air as an anchor right away, your best bet is radio news.

How about starting in radio and moving to television after a year or two? Radio can give solid experience in writing, on-air delivery, interviewing, first-hand reporting and the live, 'on your feet' reporting of spot news that's central to both radio and TV news. Radio provides good experience for either medium. Some TV news directors hire reporters from radio stations in their area because they know the area much better in contrast to an outsider. Others are so visually oriented that they prefer people who have worked in television from the start. It depends on the station.

What should be the motto: to be a specialist or a generalist? Beware of becoming a specialist too soon. The ability to do most of the jobs in a news operation adds to career flexibility and your long-term credentials, particularly in the management track. A drawback in starting one's career in a major television setup is getting pegged down and stuck in a low-level inside job when you would prefer to be out reporting. Those big operations usually get their reporters, not from the ranks of their own desk assistants, but from reporters who have gained experience in smaller markets.

Versatility cannot be over-emphasised. It is best developed in a small or medium operation where you can report, write, go on the air and take part in the production of stories. The smaller the staff, the greater the variety of things you are likely to do. Learn to add a multi-faceted skill set in your profile while trying out positions and disbursing various on-the-job duties to see which fit best for your later specialisation. Most reporters at the station level are on general assignments and thus regularly cover all kinds of news as part of their duty. In large organisations however, there are specialists in such areas as business, consumer affairs and health. Veteran specialised reporters tend to be among the best paid.

The small-market radio news director is a generalist, often a one-person band who keeps up with the community, gathers news, writes it, edits tape and goes on the air as a newscaster.

## Going After that Entry Job

Start looking for a job early in your final term of college. You may have developed job leads or made contacts much before. But there is usually no point in applying for a job until you are within a few weeks of being ready to go to work. Most openings need filling promptly.

**Cover all bases:** Use your college/institution placement service. Watch job openings bulletin boards. Check ads in trade publications. Keep in touch with your professors, who may hear of openings.

**Focus:** How selective should you be in applying? It earns a varied opinion. You may be counselled to take the shotgun approach and apply everywhere, just in case. But I would advise limiting yourself to stations that are realistic prospects. Make a concentrated effort with those stations. Do your homework. Learn the news director's name. Learn the station's programme format, coverage area and news philosophy. You can then tailor your application to that station. If there is one where you would particularly like to work, visit it if possible. Even if there is no opening at the time, ask to come by to see the operation because you are interested as a new journalist. You may also make valuable contacts.

**Letter:** Your job application letter should be businesslike, to the point and targeted to the individual news director. Try to hold it to one page. Describe why you want the job, what you have to offer and when you would be available. If applying for a television job that may involve on-air reporting, inform that a video of your work is available. If it is radio, enclose an audio CD. If the tape is unsolicited and you want it returned, enclose a stamped return envelope.

**Resumé:** Keep your resumé relevant, direct, concise and forthright. List only education, work experience and activities that bear upon the job. That can usually be done in one page. You will sell yourself best by being totally honest and humble and avoiding exaggeration. Don't mislead while describing your credentials. For example, an unpaid summer internship should be clearly listed as such and not made to sound as if you had held a full-time paying job at the station.

**Resumé tape:** Accumulate tapes or CD's of your work as evidence of how you come across on the air and put together a 'resumé tape' to be sent on request to stations where you apply for a job. Reports from the scene, especially live feeds, tell most about your potential as a reporter. Include a sample of your news casting for radio. That goes well for television too, since it can indicate potential, but don't put it at the head of your tape. If the television news director is looking for a reporter, what counts most is how well you report from a news scene.

Even if you have no tapes of stories used on the air, you can still record examples of how you perform as a reporter and newscaster. Just mention it for the convenience of prospective employer that they are lab examples.

Skip gimmicks such as using part of the tape to tell the news director how great you are. Remember your work should speak for itself. News directors have limited time for auditioning tapes, so hold yours to no more than 10-15 minutes. Put your best work, ideally field reporting for most applicants, up front. A strong lead can help keep you from getting written off within one minute.

184

Make multiple copies of your audio or video resume tape. A few stations may want to keep yours on file for future consideration. Make it easy for others to return the tape, but don't expect all of them to do so. Many tapes, unsolicited ones in particular, wind up in wastebaskets or recycling bins.

Remember landing up with a desired job may take time. Don't be surprised if several weeks or months and many rejections go by before you get a job. It is a very competitive line. But if you really believe you have what it takes, keep trying. Hanging in demonstrates that you have one of the qualities of a good journalist, which is persistence.

## 10. I am thinking of a career change. What do you suggest?

Well, for starters, the grass often looks greener on the other side here and it seems a good breakthrough for another career. Lawyers, teachers and others normally may think they should rather be working in broadcast news. At the same time, broadcast journalists may feel a need to change, perhaps to become lawyers, teachers, public relations practitioners, etc. In today's workplace, people feel less locked in than they used to. One theory is that the average worker will hold half a dozen different kinds of job profiles in the course of his lifetime. So the 'ins and outs' of broadcast journalism are not unusual.

**Moving In**

Job satisfaction is high among broadcast journalists. Not surprisingly, the field has great appeal for many when viewed from the outside. People who would like to be out there in the middle of the thick of things, who want their work to make a difference, who simply like communicating, or who have the mistaken notion that most of those television and radio jobs surely pay well are included in the list who want to change in to this profession. They generally conjecture what it would take to get into electronic journalism. Just knocking on doors? Going back to college? Well, it depends on the person, his or her work experience and his capabilities.

185

From within mass media. Convergence is bringing greater overlap among print, television, radio and web journalism. A person may work in two or three media in a single shift.

Moving from print to electronic media is not uncommon. An experienced newspaper reporter should already have the news know-how and would need to adapt mainly to on-camera reporting, often working without a script or even notes. Practice and perhaps some coaching can help. A broadcast journalism skill course at a nearby university may also be an option. Realistically, keep in mind that some people have more on-air potential than others.

An adaptable newspaper managing editor working behind the scenes here may go to a comparable job in television or radio.

A master's degree in broadcast journalism may still be the way to go, especially if print experience is slight. Advanced education is more than just skills training and generally counts long-term, whatever one's career route.

**From outside mass media:** Now what of someone with no journalism education or experience? How about a lawyer going to TV news?

A number of the reporters and anchors seen on broadcast and cable networks are lawyers who made that move. Those with courtroom experience have practice in thinking and talking unscripted, spontaneously and persuasively while on their feet. For television, they may need to learn only the basics of journalism, which shares many elements with law such as effective communication and working in public affairs. News handling can be learned on the job.

But a master's degree in broadcast journalism might still help. A master's degree is usually recommended to all those who want to get into TV journalism and who have the potential.

## B. Ghost writer and Ghost writing

### 11. What does a ghost writer do?

A ghost writer is a skilled writer who collaborates with an author needing help in turning a book idea into a finished piece of work. Ghost writers are commonly employed in many fields of journalism as well as book publishing, which includes their active involvement in both fiction and non-fiction. In fact, at any given time, a large fraction of the books on national bestseller lists are likely to be products of an author/ghost writer relationship.

The collaboration between an author and a ghost writer may take several forms. Sometimes, the author creates a draft manuscript that the ghost writer thoroughly rewrites, perhaps adding and discarding sections as well as reorganising the sequence of materials. (A less-extensive revision shades into 'editing' rather than ghost writing; there is no precise rule as to where the line is drawn.)

In other cases, the ghost writer will interview the author extensively and write a manuscript based on information, ideas and stories drawn from those interviews. In the case of a non-fiction work, the ghost writer may also interview other people and conduct other forms of research.

In some instances, the author may contribute little beyond the basic idea; the ghost writer is responsible for virtually the entire intellectual and literary content of the book, and the author is a mere 'figurehead', often a celebrity whose name will help to market the book.

The form of authorship credit received by the ghost writer also varies. Sometimes, the ghost writer remains completely invisible, with only a mention on the author's acknowledgements page (perhaps described as an 'editor' or 'adviser').

## 12. What are the problems faced by ghost writers?

**Cooperation:** One of the biggest problems that a ghost writer faces often is obtaining access to and cooperation by the person commissioning the work. The ghost writer's task will obviously be much more difficult if he or she has to conduct substantial research, organise or verify large amounts of information, or struggle to get sufficient interview time with the author. There can be perplexing and Herculean problems if the author has a right of approval over the ghost writer's work. This is particularly true if the work is an autobiography. The author may wish to deviate from reality in depicting certain events in his or her life, while the ghost writer may feel obligated to report these events as they actually occurred.

**Copyright:** The author and the ghost writer may agree to treat the work as a joint work, or the author may require the ghost writer to assign all of his or her rights in the work to the author. In the former situation, the author and the ghost writer will be equal co-owners of the copyright in the work, and unless they agree otherwise, both will have to consent to all publications and other uses of the work. In the latter situation, the author will be the sole owner of the copyright in the work, and the ghost writer will not have any control over the use of the work, or any modifications to the work. If the author requires an assignment of copyright from the ghost writer, the ghost writer may decide not to be credited, since he or she will not have any say over the final form of the work.

**Compensation:** The ghost writer may receive payment in the form of a one-time fixed fee, a share of royalties, or some combination of the two. In addition, the ghost writer may be entitled to some portion of the author's proceeds if the book is licensed for other uses, such as a movie, television show or stage play. If the ghost writer's compensation is to be based solely on royalties from publication, the ghost writer may want a guaranteed payment in the event the work cannot be completed or published due to delays or other problems caused by the author.

**Credit:** A ghost writer working on the biography of a celebrity or similar work will often receive credit in the form of 'with' or 'as told to'. However, ghost writers of other types of books, such as books by business consultants or seminar presenters, usually will not be credited, since one of the purposes of creating such a book is to gain attention and publicity for the author as an accomplished expert in his or her field.

Ghost writing can provide a valuable service to a would-be author and a lucrative source of income for a writer. However, before beginning a project, the author and the ghost writer should make sure that they share the same vision and expectations for the project. Once this has been established, they should enter into an agreement to serve as a road map for their relationship.

## C. Radio Jockeys

### 13. What do Disc Jockeys or Radio Jockeys do?

Disc jockeys, also known as 'radio deejays,' put music on the radio. These announcers make a selection of songs and numbers that are played and announce them. They also talk about news, sports and weather. Sometimes they also do commercials, stage guest shows and tell what is going on in the community.

### 14. What is the job profile of a radio jockey?

Disc jockeys most often work at radio stations. They work in small rooms called studios. These rooms have good light, air-conditioning, and are soundproof. But it can be lonely. Full-time disc jockeys talk on the radio 5 or 6 days a week for about 4 hours at a time. However, their job takes more time than just that. Every day they must prepare for the radio show. Sometimes they write the commercials, too.

Most radio stations are on the air for long durations. Some stations broadcast their services for the whole of 24 hours every day. Because of this, disc jockeys don't usually work regular hours. They often must start early or work late into the night. They also must get to work, whatever problems they encounter, be it weather or any other spoilsport. Disc jockeys may also work outside the station. They can work at schools or community events.

## 15. How do I prepare for this job?

It is very difficult to exactly state as to how one should prepare for this job. Classes in broadcast journalism at the college may help. Courses in English, Public Speaking, and Drama are also favourable options. However, most employers would wish to ascertain the sound and diction of their jockey through a taped audition before making any commitment because the quality of the aired voice creates their brand. They pay a lot of attention to a person's way of talking. They want someone with a pleasant voice and good positive approach with a lot of presence of mind. They also prefer a disc jockey who will do commercials, news, and interviews with an attractive style.

It is therefore imminent that a disc jockey can do a lot of glib talk and 'ad-lib' that is talk without making notes on all or a part of the programme. They must work under tight deadlines and may have to be computer-literate.

Beginners often must start out in another radio job. The best chance for a disc jockey job is at a small local station.

□□□

# Journalism as a Career

Journalism is a fascinating profession. Whether your interest in the business of writing is limited to reporting for a newspaper or whether you are looking towards a lifetime career in the world of publications, you can gain a great deal from the professional contacts that are open to you.

Why not consider Journalism as a career then?

Newspaper work is challenging and exciting. There is the satisfaction that comes from service to a community and from actually getting published. Newspaper people are devoted to their profession. Above all, they like to write and report. Opportunities for beginners are good, promotions usually come regularly and salaries are generally high. In return, the profession requires hard work and willingness to accept responsibility.

The field of journalism is constantly expanding beyond the fundamental horizons of the concept of newspaper itself. Even within the newspaper, there are opportunities in news reporting, editorial work, business management, advertising, circulation and technical production. Wire services, syndicates, magazines and trade or professional journals offer similar work opportunities. Numerous other types of journalists are associated with it, namely, freelance writers, radio or television writers and editors, public relations workers and writers, advertising copywriters, photo journalists, technical writers; the list is virtually endless.

There are almost as many different ways of getting started in journalism, as there are jobs in this field. In general, a broad college education in liberal arts is recommended. You should add some basic technical training in writing and editorial work, such as that offered by college journalism programmes. If courses in Journalism are not available at the college you attend, you can work on college publications, write for local newspapers or participate in some other journalistic activity in which you must write intensively and meet rigorous standards.

The following sections enlist various universities that endeavour to improve journalistic skills and attract talented young people into this field.

## Diploma in Journalism

**Duration: 1 Year**

**Minimum qualification: Graduation in any discipline**

1. Aligarh Muslim University, Aligarh – 202 001

2. Garhwal University, Srinagar – 246 174 UP

3. Alagappa University, Alagappa Nagar, Karaikudi – 623 004 (Tamil Nadu)

4. Indian Institute of Mass Communications, New Delhi

5. Osmania University, Hyderabad – 440 001

## Graduation Courses

**Duration: 3 Years**

**Minimum qualification: 10+2 in any stream**

1. Bombay University, M. G. Road, Fort, Mumbai – 400 032

2. South Gujarat University, P. B. No. 49, Udhna – Magdalla Road, Surat – 395 007

3. Himachal Pradesh University, Shimla – 171 005

4. Bangalore University, Bangalore – 560 056

5. Marathwada University, Aurangabad – 431 004

6. Benaras Hindu University, Varanasi – 221 005

7. University of Calcutta, Kolkata – 700 073

8. Lalit Narayan Mithila University, Kameeshwarnagar – 840 004.

9. Manipur University, Imphal – 795 003

10. Delhi University, New Delhi

## Masters Degree

**Duration: 2 Years**

**Minimum qualification: Graduation**

1. Punjab University, Patiala – 147 002

2. Benaras Hindu University, Varanasi – 221 005

3. Jamia Millia Islamia, Jamia Nagar, New Delhi – 110 025.

## Diploma in Photography

1. University of Allahabad, Allahabad – 221 002

2. University of Gorakhpur, Gorakhpur – 273 001

3. Jawaharlal Nehru Technological University, Hyderabad – 500 028

## Post-Graduate Diploma in Advertising

1. Indian Institute of Mass Communications, New Delhi

2. Rajendra Prasad Institute of Communication and Management, Mumbai

3. Madurai Kamraj University, Vivekananda College, Tiruvedakam West, Tamil Nadu

4. University of Madras, Madras Christian College, Chennai

5. School for Communication and Management Studies, Thevar House, Cochin – 682 133

6. Karnataka University, B. V. V. Basaveshwar Commerce College, Bagalkot

7. University of Bombay, Jai H. College of Arts and JT Lalwani College of Commerce, Mumbai

8. University of Poona, Department of Communication and Journalism, Gokhale Education Society, Nasik

9. Dibrugarh University, JB College, Jorhat

10. Magadha University, Gaya College, Gaya

Some of the institutions listed above also offer degree programme in advertising.

□□□

# Glossary

**Advance story:** News story about an event published before the event is scheduled to take place.

**Advertisement:** Space in a newspaper paid for by someone who has goods or services to sell.

**Assignment:** deputing a reporter to cover a specific news story.

**Assignment book (Assignment sheet):** Listing of reporters' assignments, kept by the editor or news editor.

**Balance:** Arrangement of items on a newspaper page so that stories and pictures on one section of the page balance as evenly as possible with masses of type on the opposite section.

**Bank:** In case of journalism, and especially printing, a bank is a place where typeset copy (filler, stories held over from an issue) is stored for future use.

**Banner (Streamer):** Headline that extends across the page.

**Beat (Run):** Place or source a reporter covers regularly to get news.

**Blind interview:** Interview granted by a person in authority on condition that his name be withheld.

**Body:** All of a news story after the lead paragraph.

**Body type:** Type in which all material other than ads is set.

**Boil down:** Shorten.

**Boldface:** Heavy black letters.

| | |
|---|---|
| Sanjana | **Sanjana** |
| ↓ | ↓ |
| Normal | Boldface |
| *Sanjana* | **Sanjana** |
| ↓ | ↓ |
| Italic Reverse | |

**Box:** Lines around a printed story or headline.

**Box score:** Statistical summary of a sports event usually printed in small type at the end of a news story.

**Break:** The point in a column where a story is divided, to be continued on another page; also, to release a story for publication.

**Bulletin:** Brief but important statement of last-minute news.

**By-line:** Small printed name below the headline, crediting the writer of a story, as "By Sanjana…"

**Caps (Upper case):** Capital letters

**Caption (Cutline, Legend):** Paragraph appearing below a cut, describing the illustration.

**Catch line:** One or two words which identify a piece of copy.

**Censorship:** Control by legally designated authority (usually governmental or religious) of what is said or written.

**Chronological order:** Arrangement of events in the order in which they took place or are scheduled to take place.

**Circulation:** Average total number of copies of a newspaper distributed per issue; also, the process of distributing a newspaper to its readers.

**Clean copy:** Written material containing relatively few errors and thus requiring little or no editing.

**Cliché:** A once-colourful phrase that has been used so many times that it is no longer effective.

**Column:** An article under a permanent title, written regularly by the same person, giving expression to his own opinion; also, a vertical row of type on a printed page.

**Column inch:** Space measurement: one vertical inch, one column wide.

**Columnist:** Writer who regularly has a column appearing in a newspaper or distributed by a newspaper syndicate.

**Column rule:** Printed line used to divide two columns.

**Commentary:** Interpretation of news by a qualified observer (commentator).

**Community:** Group of people who live in the same geographic area, share the same public and commercial services, and have similar interests.

**Compact:** Newspaper with pages approximately 11 × 15 inches, like the tabloid, but with more conservative format.

**Composite news story:** News story with more than one key thought, or dealing with more than a single event.

**Composition:** Photographer's arrangement of subjects to produce an eye-appealing picture.

**Contrast:** Use of varied font styles, sizes and types to make each story stand out according to its relative importance.

**Copy:** Any written material that is to be put into type.

**Copydesk:** Table at which copyreaders work, often semicircular in shape; the city editor may sit in the slot at the centre.

**Copy fitting:** Adjusting or rewriting copy to make it fit the space allotted.

**Copyholder:** Person who reads copy aloud so that a proofreader may check a proof for errors.

**Copyreader:** Person who corrects and improves copy submitted by reporters.

**Copyreaders' marks:** Universal system of symbols by which copyreaders indicate corrections to be made in copy.

**Copyright:** Author's or artist's right to control publication of his original work.

**Cover a story:** Secure all available facts about a news event.

**Credit Line:** A line stating the source of a story or picture.

**Crop:** Eliminating unwanted details in a picture by marking off those areas that are not to be included.

**Cross line:** Headline pattern of a single line extending full column width.

**Cub reporter:** An inexperienced newspaper reporter.

**Cut-off rule:** Line extending completely across a column, above or below a story.

**Cut-off test:** Test applied to a newspaper story to determine if the last paragraphs contain any essential facts.

**Dateline:** Date and place of origin, printed at the beginning of a news story.

**Deadline:** Final time by when all ad copy and stories are due to be submitted for publication.

**Dead:** Term used to describe material set in type but not used, or no longer suitable for use.

**Deck:** One in a series of headlines above a single story.

**Depth of field:** In photography, measure of distance, in front of and beyond the subject focused upon, within which details will be acceptably sharp.

**Display:** Use of headlines and arrangement of pictures and copy on a page to make it easy to find and read a story.

**Down style:** Newspaper style capitalising as few words as possible. Up style is the opposite.

**Dropline (Step head):** Headline pattern consisting of two or more lines with a slanting appearance, the first line touching the left margin only, the last line touching the right margin only.

**Dummy:** Sketch of the way a page will look, showing the printer where each ad, story and picture is to be placed.

**Ears:** Small boxes placed at the sides of the nameplate, containing brief messages or bits of information.

**Editor:** Person in charge of putting out a newspaper, or a section of a newspaper.

**Editorial:** Article stating the opinion of a newspaper publisher or editor.

**Editorial campaign:** Concerted effort by a newspaper staff to promote an idea by using all the resources of the newspaper as well as other media.

**Editorial page:** Page containing editorials, columns and special material, usually of a serious nature.

**Editorial policy:** Statement of a newspaper's purpose or goals. It is also the paper's official policy in regard to controversial and other topics in the news.

**Editorial 'We':** First person plural pronoun, referring to the newspaper's publisher or editor, used only in editorials.

**Editorial writer:** On the payrolls of large daily newspapers, staff member whose main duty it is to write editorials.

**Eye movement:** Movement of reader's eyes from one article or feature to another on a page.

**Eyewitness reporting:** Gathering material for a news story by actually being present at an event such as a meeting, sports competition or accident.

**Feature:** News story written in an informal way; a story that provides information or entertainment.

**Filler:** A story or brief informational matter that may be used at any time to fill space in a column or page.

**Floating nameplate:** Nameplate that may appear in various positions on a page in succeeding issues.

**Fold:** Imaginary horizontal line across the centre of a newspaper page.

**Follow up:** Story giving new information on news previously published.

**Font:** A complete set of type of one size and design, include alphabets in caps and lower case letters plus numerals and special symbols.

**Format:** Physical size and makeup of a newspaper.

**Future Book:** List of all stories of known future events for coming issues of the newspaper.

**Gang:** Assemble similar material (photos or display) in a single group.

**Hanging indentation:** Headline pattern in which the first line touches the left margin but succeeding lines are indented.

**Headline schedule:** Printed examples of a newspaper's various headline patterns.

**Horizontal makeup:** Makeup style that uses many headlines, cuts and stories extending across two or more columns.

**Horizontal units:** Stories under multicolumn heads used partly to break up long, single, vertical columns.

**Human interest:** News element that deals with people and their entertaining or unusual actions, particularly those appealing to the emotions.

**Indent:** Set type at a certain distance from the margin.

**Interview:** Get facts for a news story by talking with an individual. Also, the written story based on this conversation.

**Inverted pyramid:** Normal arrangement for the body of a news story, in which the facts are placed in descending order of their news value.

**Inverted pyramid head:** A headline pattern in which each succeeding line is shorter than the preceding line.

**Italics:** Slanted letters.

**Journalism:** Process of collecting, writing, editing and publishing news.

**Journalist:** Person, who collects, writes or edits news.

**Jump:** To break a story on one page and continue it elsewhere.

**Jump head:** Headline used on a story continued from another page. It repeats key words from the original headline.

**Justification:** Spacing out type so that lines fit the right-hand margin evenly.

**Key thought:** Most important fact in a news story.

**Kicker (also Astonished Read-in, Tag line, Whiplash):** Short headline in small type usually placed flush left and above a main head.

**Killed:** Deleted before publication

**Lead (Pronounced Leed):** First paragraph of a news story, giving a summary of the entire story.

**Legman:** Person who collects information and transmits it to a staff member, usually a rewrite man, for writing.

**Libel:** Spoken or written statement that unjustly damages someone's reputation or exposes him to ridicule.

**Makeup:** Principles for arranging a newspaper page. A layout is the plan for arrangement of copy, headlines, illustrations and advertisements as they appear on a finished page. A dummy is the sketch or paste-up of a page. To make a page is to arrange the stories on the actual page.

**Mass communication:** Distribution of printed or spoken words, pictures or ideas in such a way as to reach and influence a large number of people.

**Mass media:** Instruments of mass communication; for example, books, newspapers, radio or television.

**Masthead (Flag):** Name, ownership, staff and statement of policy of a newspaper, usually appearing in a box on the editorial page. This sometimes includes circulation figures, subscription fees, and advertising rates. Also the name of the paper displayed at the top of the front page.

**Morgue:** Newspaper library.

**News peg:** A specific current event about which an editorial or feature is written.

**News-source:** Person or persons who may give information or news.

**Novelty (Unorthodox) lead:** Lead paragraph that does not follow the usual pattern.

**Obituary (Obit):** News story about a death. This generally includes biographical information.

**Offset (Photo-offset):** Printing process in which a specially processed photographic plate prints onto a rubber roller, which in turn transfers the ink to the paper.

**Over line:** Headline appearing above a cut (rarely used in streamlined newspapers).

**Page editor:** Editors whose duty it is to plan, arrange, and follow up production of one page.

**Page layout:** Plan for arrangement of copy, headlines, illustrations, and advertisements, as they are to appear on a finished page.

**Personality short:** Brief collection of pertinent facts describing an individual.

**Personality story:** News feature describing an individual.

**Plate:** Piece of metal (aluminium sheet) on which a printing image appears either in relief or in depression.

**Press Association (also Wire service):** Organisation that collects news all over the world and sends it to member newspapers. Best known here are Press Trust of India (PTI), Associated Press (AP), Reuters etc.

**Press release:** Material given to a newspaper by an organisation or person seeking publicity.

**Promotion:** An advertising campaign based on a single event or idea and using tie-in ads.

**Proof:** Print made of a story as soon as it is set in type.

**Proofreader:** Person who compares proof with copy and makes necessary corrections.

**Proofreaders' marks:** Universal system of symbols by which proofreaders indicate corrections; they differ from copyreaders' marks.

**Propaganda:** Written or spoken material designed to influence thought or action.

**Prospect:** A business firm that may be interested in advertising in a newspaper.

**Publicity:** Newsworthy information issued to gain public attention or support.

**Public relations:** Activities of an organisation to build and maintain productive relations with the public so as to interpret itself favourably to society.

**Publisher:** Owner or manager of the magazine, book or newspaper business.

**Put the paper to bed:** Complete all checking so that the paper is ready for publication.

**Pyramid:** Arrangement of ads on a page (usually half-pyramid in shape, from lower-left corner to upper-right corner).

**Reporter:** Person who gathers news and usually writes the news story.

**Review:** Critical discussion, usually about an event in the field of entertainment.

**Rewrite man:** In a daily newspaper office, the man who takes legmen's stories over the telephone and writes them for the paper.

**Running head (Folio line):** Line or two of font on each page of newspaper, identifying the page number and date; it may include additional information about the paper.

**Scale:** Enlarge or reduce a photograph so that it will fit a desired space on a page.

**Scoop:** Exclusive story or one published before other news media release it.

**Serif:** Small decorative line across the end of a stroke used in forming a letter. This letter has serifs: K. Sans serif is a font without serifs: K.

**Sidebar:** Secondary story presenting sidelights on a major news story.

**Slant:** Write or place a story intentionally or unintentionally, in such a way that the reader misjudges its truth or importance.

**Sports advance:** News story, discussion or a sports event scheduled to take place in the future.

**Sports report:** News story about a sports event, generally by a reporter who has personally witnessed the event.

**Sports summary:** News story or informative news feature covering a series of sports events or a complete sports season.

**Spot news:** Unexpected news, reported immediately.

**Spread:** Headline across two or three columns; also, two facing pages.

**Stale news:** News so old that readers are not interested in it.

**Standard news lead:** Lead paragraph of a news story that presents the facts in simple, direct language.

**Stet:** Proofreader's mark meaning to restore crossed-out words or letters; usually written in the margin with dots under the words or letters to be kept.

**String book:** Reporter's collection of his printed stories.

**Style sheet:** Set of rules governing writing style. Most newspapers set up their own preferred style.

**Subhead:** One-line headline, usually in boldface type, between paragraphs of a story.

**Summary lead:** Introductory paragraph containing most of the main points in a story.

**Symposium:** Collection of many people's answers to the same question.

**Syndicate:** Company that buys feature material from writers and sells it to newspapers.

**Tabloid:** Newspaper with five-column pages, approximately half the size of standard eight-column page, and frequently with streamlined makeup.

**Thumbnail cut:** ½ column cut.

**Tie-in:** Topic used as a purpose or theme for interviewing a particular individual.

**Tip:** Suggestion for a possible news story.

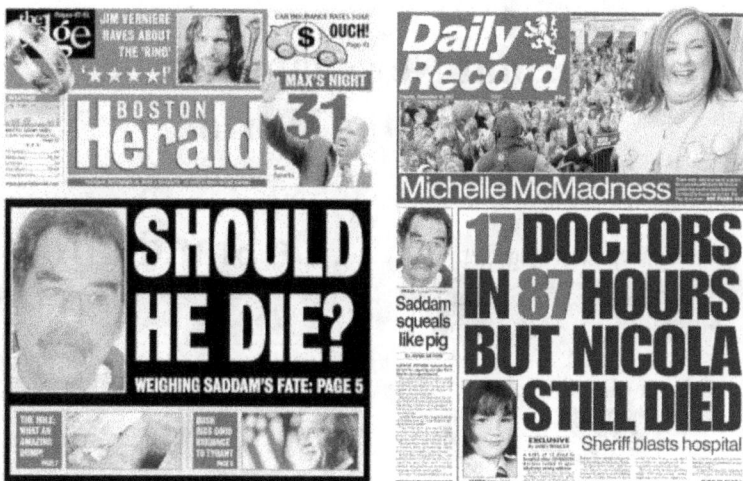

*Tabloids*

**Tomb stoning:** Use of similar headlines in adjoining columns.

**Widow:** A final line in a paragraph, containing a single word or less than half a line of type, and appearing at the top or bottom of a type page or column.

Wooden headline: Head that is little more than a label.

□□□

# Important Newspapers from Around the World

**The Sydney Morning Herald**

**Australia** – The Sydney Morning Herald

**De Standaard**

**Belgium** – De Standaard

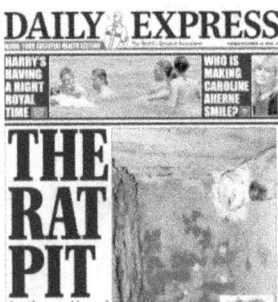

**DAILY EXPRESS**

**Britain** – Daily Express

**Tribunal deve vetar revisão automática do INSS**

**Brazil** – Agora

**CHINA DAILY**

**China** – China Daily

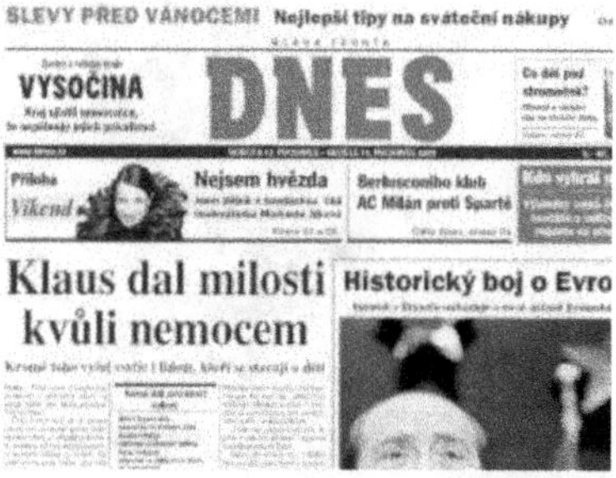
SLEVY PŘED VÁNOCEMI Nejlepší tipy na sváteční nákupy
VYSOČINA
DNES
Nejsem hvězda
Berlusconiho klub AC Milán proti Spartě
Klaus dal milosti kvůli nemocem
Historický boj o Evro

**Czech Republic** – Dnes

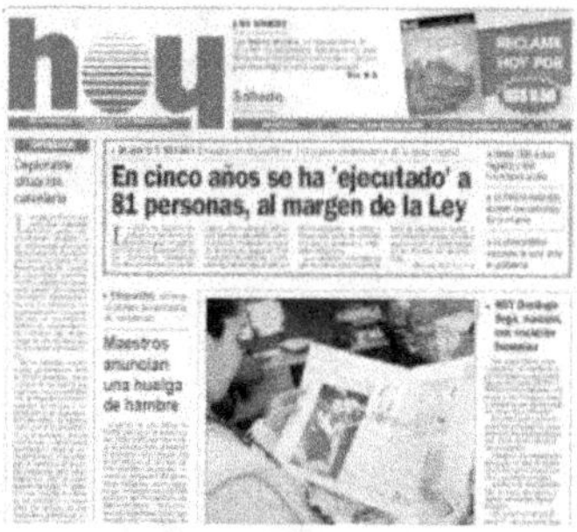
hoy
En cinco años se ha 'ejecutado' a 81 personas, al margen de la Ley
Maestros anuncian una huelga de hambre

**Ecuador** – Hoy

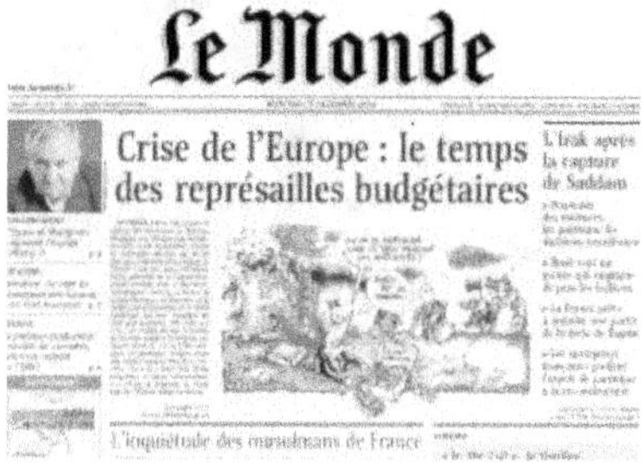
Le Monde
Crise de l'Europe : le temps des représailles budgétaires
L'Irak après la capture de Saddam
L'inquiétude des musulmans de France

**France** – Le Monde

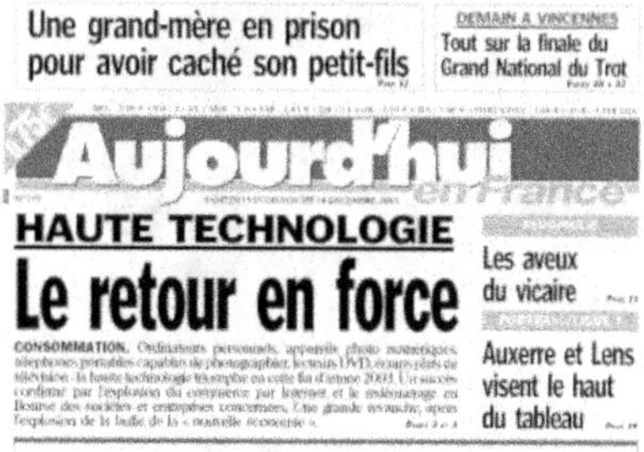
Une grand-mère en prison pour avoir caché son petit-fils
DEMAIN À VINCENNES
Tout sur la finale du Grand National du Trot
Aujourd'hui en France
HAUTE TECHNOLOGIE
Le retour en force
Les aveux du vicaire
Auxerre et Lens visent le haut du tableau

**France** – Aujourd'hui

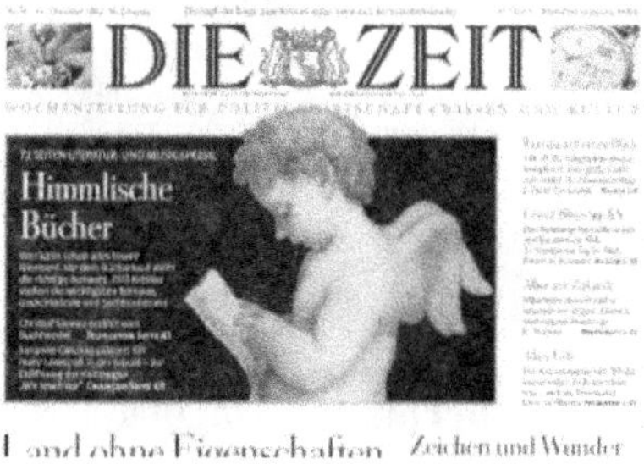
DIE ZEIT
Himmlische Bücher
Land ohne Eigenschaften
Zeichen und Wunder

**Germany** – Die Zeit

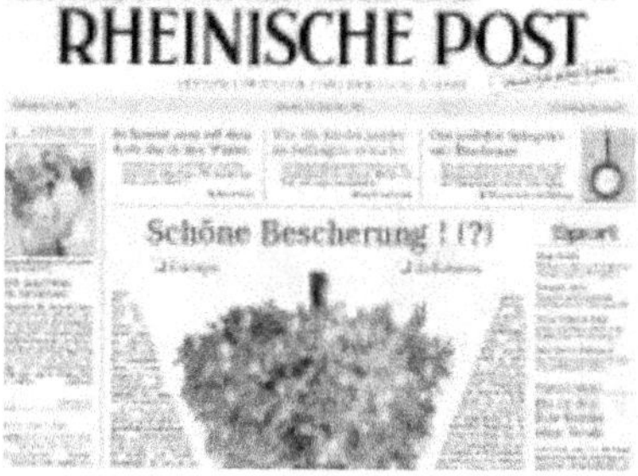
RHEINISCHE POST
Schöne Bescherung ! (?)

**Germany** – Rheinische Post

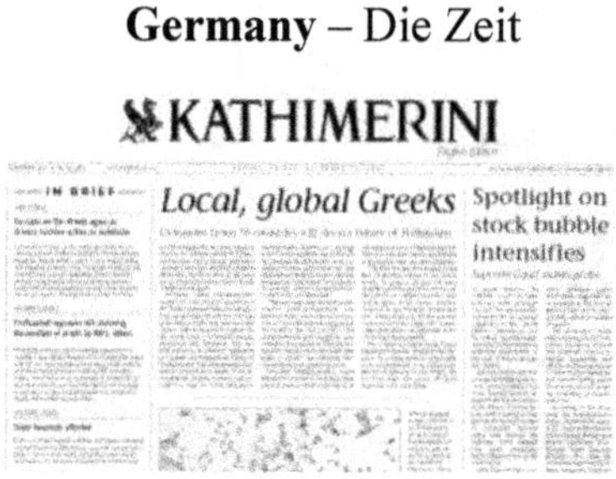
KATHIMERINI
IN BRIEF
Local, global Greeks
Spotlight on stock bubble intensifies

**Greece** – Kathimerini

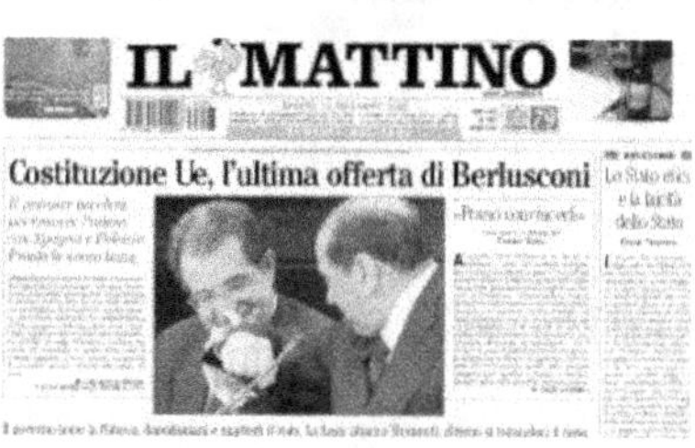
IL MATTINO
Costituzione Ue, l'ultima offerta di Berlusconi

**Italy** – IL Mattino

**Iceland** – Morgunbladid

**Japan** – Okinawa Times

**Israel** – The Jerusalem Post

**Japan** – Sports Nippon

**Lebanon** – Al Mustaqbal

**Netherlands** – Dagblad

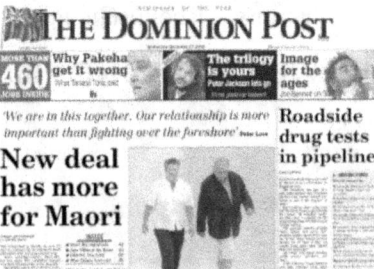
**New Zealand** – The Dominion Post

**Norway** – Dagbladet

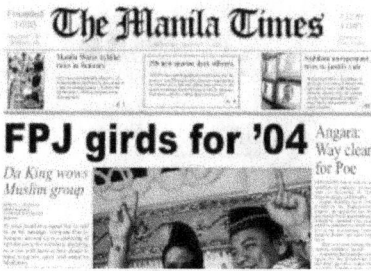

**Philippines** – The Manila Times

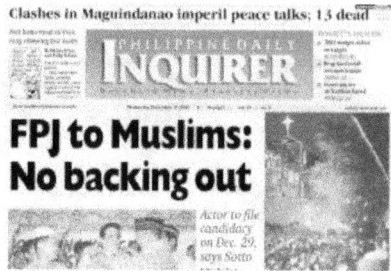

**Philippines** –
Philippine Daily Inquirer

**Poland** – Gazeta Wyborcza

**Russia** – Moscow News

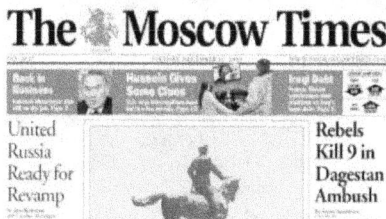

**Russia** – The Moscow Times

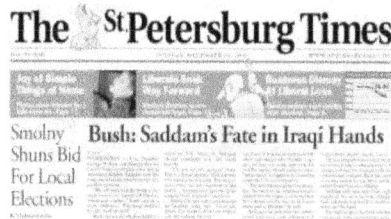

**Russia** – The St. Petersburg Times

**Saudi Arabia** – Al Eqtisidiah

**Slovenia** – Delo Fax

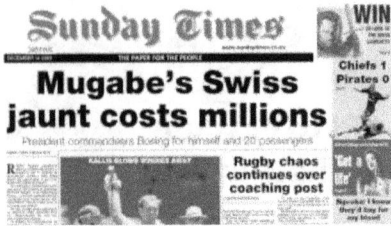

**South Africa** – Sunday Times

**Spain** – Expansión

**Spain** – Marca

**Sweden** – Kvällsposten

**Switzerland** – Basler Zeitung

**Switzerland** – Le Temps

**Turkey** – Hurriyet

**Ukraine** – Kiyevskiy Telegraph

**USA** – USA Today

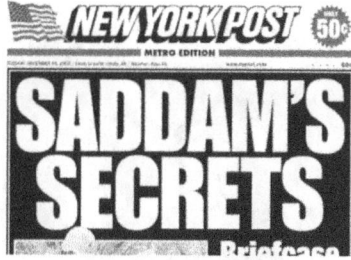

**USA** – New York Post

**USA** – The Washington Times

**India** – Dinamalar

**India** – Udayavani

**India** – Hindustan Times

**India** – The Economic Times

**India** – The Times of India

# Bibliography

Anonymous (1996): "The Press: Code for Owners", Economic and Political Weekly, Vol. 31, No. 5: 245.

Anonymous (1998): "Media Ethics: Down-Turn", Economic and Political Weekly, Vol. 33, No. 18: 997.

Arora, Sushil (1992): "The Audio-Visual Media and a Research Potential", Man in India, Vol. 72, No. 1: 55-63.

Bathla, Sonia (1998): Women, Democracy and the Media: Cultural and Political Representations in the Indian Press. New Delhi: Sage Publications.

Bhaskar, Manu (1989): Press and Working Class Consciousness in Developing Societies. A Case Study of an Indian State – Kerala. New Delhi: Gian Publishing House.

Chakravorti, Robi (1994): "Indian, Pakistan and the US Media", Economic and Political Weekly. Vol. 29, No. 26: 1583-1584.

Chauhan, Swati & Chandra, Navin (1997): Journalism Today: Principles, Practices and Challenges. Vol. 1: Modern Journalism: Issues and Approaches. New Delhi: Kanishka Publishers.

Chick, John (1996): "Cecil King, the Press, and Politics in West Africa", The Journal of Modern African Studies.Vol. 34, No. 3: 375-395.

Dharker, Anil (1997): Sorry, Not Ready: Television in the Time of PMdarshan. New Delhi: HarperCollins Publishers India.

Donway, Roger & Kelley, David (1990): "Liberalism and Free Speech", in Judith Lichtenberg (ed.), Democracy and the Mass Media: A Collection of Essays. Cambridge: Cambridge University Press.

Dorkenoo, Bernard D. (1989): "Press Freedom is Key to Realization of Human Rights in Africa", in Asbjørn Eide & Sigrun Skogly (eds.), Human Rights and the Media. Oslo: Norwegian Institute of Human Rights Publications.

D'Souza, Y. K. (1998): Freedom of Press, Constitution and Media Responsibility. New Delhi: Commonwealth Publishers.

Dunnett, P. J. S. (1988): The World Newspaper Industry. London: Croom Helm.

Eide, Asbjørn (1989): "The Media and International Human Rights – an Imperfect Partnership" in Asbjørn Eide & Sigrun Skogly (eds.), Human Rights and the Media. Oslo: Norwegian Institute of Human Rights Publications.

Farmer, Victoria (1996): "Mass Media: Images, Mobilisation, and Communalism", Chapter 4 in David Ludden (ed.), Contesting the Nation: Religion, Community, and the Politics of Democracy in India. Philadelphia: University of Pennsylvania Press.

Freedom House (1997): Press Freedom 1996: The Journalist as Pariah, Leonard R. Sussman, (ed.). Gurevitch, Michael & Blumler, Jay G. (1990): "Political Communication Systems and Democratic values", in Judith Lichtenberg (ed.), Democracy and the Mass Media: A Collection of Essays. Cambridge: Cambridge University Press.

Hohenberg, John (1971): Free Press / Free People: The Best Cause. New York: Columbia University Press.

Iyer, V. R. Krishna (1994): "Foreign Print Media Incarnating as Indian Fourth Estate?" Economic and Political Weekly, December 1994: 3082-3085.

Joseph, Ammu & Sharma, Kalpana (eds.) (1994): Whose News? The Media and Women's Issues. New Delhi: Sage Publications.

Kasoma, Francis P. (1994): "Participatory Rural Newspapers as Agents of Development: A Reciprocal Agenda- Setting Model", in Shirley A. White with K. Sadanandan Nair & Joseph Ascroft (eds.), Participatory Communication: Working for Change and Development. New Delhi: Sage Publications.

Kuppuswamy, B. (1975): "The Expansion in Mass Media", chapter 18 in Social Change in India. Delhi: Vikas Publishing House.

Manoff, Richard K. (1973): "The Mass Media Contributions to Intervention Programs", in Alan Berg, Nevin S. Scrimshaw & David L. Call (eds.), Nutrition, National Development, and Planning: Proceedings of an International Conference held at Cambridge, Massachusetts, October 19-21, 1971. Cambridge, Mass.: The Massachusetts Institute of Technology.

Newcomb, T. M. (1958): "Communicative Behaviour", in Roland Young (ed.), Approaches to the Study of Politics: Twenty-two Contemporary Essays Exploring the Nature of Politics and Methods by Which it Can Be Studied. Evanston, Illinois: Northwestern University Press.

Parashar, Rajesh (1994): Public Service Television. Values and Interests at Stake: A Study of Development of Media Politics in Norway and India. Bergen: Department of Mass Communication, University of Bergen.

Parmar, Shyam (1975): Traditional Folk Media in India. New Delhi: Geka Books.

Reporters sans frontières (1993): Freedom of the Press throughout the World: 1993 Report. London: J.Libbey.

Schramm, Wilbur (1964): Mass Media and National Development: The Role of Information in the Developing Countries. Stanford, California: Stanford University Press.

Singhal, Arvind & Rogers, Everett M. (1989): India's Information Revolution. New Delhi: Sage Publications.

Sommerlad, E. Lloyd (1966): The Press in Developing Countries. Sydney: Sydney University Press.

Sood, Rahul (1993): "Message Design in Development Communication", in K. Sadanandan Nair & Shirley A. White (eds.), Perspectives on Development Communication. New Delhi: Sage Publications.

Stepp, Carl Sessions (1990): "Access in a Post-social Responsibility Age", in Judith Lichtenberg (ed.), Democracy and the Mass Media: A Collection of Essays. Cambridge: Cambridge University Press.

Sujan, D. K. (1993): "Traditional Folk Media for Rural Development", in K. Sadanandan Nair & Shirley A. White (eds.), Perspectives on Development Communication. New Delhi: Sage Publications.

Sundaram, Navina (1979): "Thoughts on the Employment of Media in Developing Countries", in Peter Herrmann & Rainer Kabel (eds.), Media, Technology, Development: The Role of Media Adapted By Developing Countries. Berlin: Spiess.

Tatarian, Roger (1978): "News Flow in the Third World: An Overview", in Philip C. Horton (ed.), The Third World and Press Freedom. New York: Praeger Publishers.

Ungar, Sanford J. (1990): "The Role of a Free Press in Strengthening Democracy", in Judith Lichtenberg (ed.), Democracy and the Mass Media: A Collection of Essays. Cambridge: Cambridge University Press.

Verghese, George (1978): "Press Censorship under Indira Gandhi", in Philip C. Horton (ed.), The Third World and Press Freedom. New York: Praeger Publishers.

Vijaya, N. (1988): The Role of Traditional Folk Media in Rural India. Delhi: Gian Publishing House.

Vilanilam, J. V. (1993): "Basic Indicators of Development in Underdeveloped Societies: The Need for a New Approach Among Communicators", in K. Sadanandan Nair & Shirley A. White (eds.), Perspectives on Development Communication. New Delhi: Sage Publications.

Wadia, Angela (1999): Communication and Media: Studies in Ideas, Initiatives and Institutions. New Delhi: Kanishka Publishers.

Yadava, J. S. (1993): "Communication and Development: For Whom and For What?", in K. Sadanandan Nair & Shirley A. White (eds.), Perspectives on Development Communication. New Delhi: Sage Publications.

Yadava, J. S. (1993): "Development Communication and Social Structure: Methodological Thoughts", in K. Sadanandan Nair & Shirley A. White (eds.), Perspectives on Development Communication. New Delhi: Sage Publications.

□□□

www.ingramcontent.com/pod-product-compliance
Lightning Source LLC
Chambersburg PA
CBHW070418270326
41926CB00014B/2843